TO: CHAD

With You

MARINA NANI

Marina

Away from Home

THE HOTEL ALTERNATIVE

A COMPLETE GUIDE FOR HOME OWNERS AND THEIR RENTAL PROPERTIES

The Ultimate Author Boot Camp, Toronto, September 2012

London • UK
www.AwayFromHome-Book.com
Marina@AwayFromHome-Book.com

Marina Nani, Author

Lori Murphy, Book Architect
Darie Nani, Contributing Author
Michael Nani, Contributing Author
Alice Demetriad, Contributing Author

ISBN: 978-0-9573195-0-9 (Paperback)
•
ISBN 978-0-9573195-1-6 (eBook-PDF)

'I DEDICATE THIS BOOK
TO LORI MURPHY,
MY BOOK ARCHITECT
WHO GUIDED ME
WITH UNCONDITIONAL
LOVE AND KINDNESS
AND MADE IT ALL POSSIBLE.
LORI IS AN EXTRAORDINARY PERSON AT MANY LEVELS
BUT HER MENTAL POWER IS LIMITLESS:
SAME DAY,
SHE BROUGHT TO LIFE,
NOT ONLY MY FIRST BOOK,
BUT HER FIRST CHILD!
THEY ARE BOTH IN MY HEART,
TO STAY FOREVER'

MARINA NANI

THE ULTIMATE AUTHOR BOOT CAMP, SEPTEMBER, TORONTO, 2012

Foreword by Raymond Aaron

'Away from home': A Win-Win galaxy

In contrast to a passive society still suffering from late 20th century apathy, the author of Away From Home is looking forward to an active and young, mature age. The only one thing that makes a real difference in anyone's life is genuine enthusiasm certified by wisdom.

As western economies are struggling to deliver contractual obligations to its citizens and failing to maintain pension provision for a decent standard of living, she is creating her own recipe for a healthier and wealthier retirement age and can really look forward to financial freedom. Travelling in business with young kids, the author struggled while living in hotel rooms and always thought that there must be a better solution for people working away from home.

When Marina Nani moved to a foreign country, she decided to work harder than most people her age and aim for success. Twenty years after starting her journey, property investment has become her loyal ally, even during economic downturn.
Marina Nani is not frightened by the current economic situation that has shaken the globe since 2008. She is creating a new travel product in reply to consumers' needs and is doing so by implementing new concepts. She is on good terms with the recession and determined to prove to her children, friends, investors, and, actually, to you and me, that

now is best time to invest in property. In times when everybody is blaming somebody else she is saying: "I can fix this". Perhaps her circumstances, as a single but proud parent, are not unique, but her upbeat attitude can melt any challenge.

There is no limit as to how far you can go by using her business model. You have to read Away From Home to see why and how her concept is working like a charm and being the occupants of a digital planet, you can access instant benefits once you do.

Do you feel bad about getting rich? Don't, because your local community will benefit from wealthy people staying at your house and spending on local services: transport companies, local shops and markets, tourist attraction, and events.

The Hotel Alternative is a win-win galaxy while your guests are the most likely to become your marketing satellites, talking on Facebook and Twitter about their great experience when residing in your home. What makes her concept so wonderful is that your clients will return the favour by recommending you on the World Wide Web!

Raymond Aaron

NY Times Bestselling Author

www.UltimateAuthorBootcamp.com

Table of Contents

Chapter I
'Away from Home'

I.1. What is the 'Hotel Alternative'? page 2
I.2. How can I help you double your rental income? page 5
I.2. Internet driven trends of consumer choice page 9
I.3. The 'Hotel Alternative': a free ticket to serendipity page 12
I.4. Differences that make the difference page 15

Chapter II
Home owners' hot desk

II.1.When and where to invest page 21
II.2. How to choose your niche and rent right page 23
II.3. Your property pays you page 25
II.4.Knowing your market page 27

Chapter III
Pride and presentation

III.1. How to benefit from worldwide market trends page 30
III.2. Your 'Hotel Alternative' goes live! page 31
III.3. Staging your home page 35
III.4. Go boutique: room by room page 39

Chapter IV
Marketing: cocktail time

IV.1.Behind the scenes (self-assessment) page 42

IV.2. Self-marketing and free platforms page 49

IV.3. Your property on the map page 51

IV.4.The real cost of bookings (fees you should not pay) page 52

IV.5. 'Five a Day' versus the vacancy syndrome page 55

Chapter V
Renting your home through professional channels

V.1.Relocation clients living at your property page 59

V.2. Holiday makers and what they expect page 62

V.3. Needs and wants page 63

Chapter VI
Welcome to my street: 'Revenue Avenue'

VI.1. Sharing availability as a chain of trusted hotel alternative properties page 66

VI.2. Enquiries, attractive rates and unique features page 68

VI.3. Bookings, confidence and transparency page 70

VI.4. Avoid poor management page 76

Chapter VII
Owner's Back Office

VII.1. Availability calendar page 79

VII.2. Booking forms page 82

VII.3. Enquiries turning into bookings page 84

VII.4. Accepting reservations/ terms and conditions page 87

VII.5. Cancellation policy page 90

Chapter VIII
The 'Hotel Alternative': Daily

VIII.1. Work smart and dress for success page 93
VIII.2. Check in to check out: one journey page 94
VIII.3. Collecting payments: deposits versus trust page 101
VII.4. Skills and confidence page 104

Chapter IX
How to conquer Everest

IX.1. Reviews page 107
IX.2. Customers' feedback and referrals page 110
IX.3.The 'Hotel Alternative' loyalty program page 118
IX.4. Knowing for knowing page 121

Chapter X
Run your portfolio as a successful family business

X.1. First property page 125
X.2. Second property page 127
X.3. Family portfolio page 128
X.4. Succession management page 130
X.5. Your legacy for success page 132

Appendix I

Free listing platform for your rental property and a few social media tips

AI.1. Keeping the sharing spirit real! page 134
AI.2. Go live in 3 steps! page 140
AI.3.The Power of social media page 142
AI.4.Why you should go blogging page 146

Appendix II

Ask the experts

AII.1. Interview with Matt, Property Investor (UK) page 149
AII.2. Interview with Celine, International Booking Agent page 152
AII.3. Winning attributes of the top bloggers by Chris, International Blogger Authority page 155

Appendix III

Take the fear out of finance

AIII.1.Cash flow model page 156
AIII.2. Management accounts made simple page 158

Appendix IV

Don't break the red tape

AIV.1. Health and fire regulations page 162
AIV.2. Tax pages round the world page 163
A.IV.3. Useful Reports and Templates page 165

'Away from Home'

I.1. What is the 'Hotel Alternative' ?

Inspired by the distilled experience of some of the world's leading entrepreneurs the content of my book has been compiled with the belief that thousands of people who invest in property will be trained to become financially free. I hope to inspire and help property investors to enhance their profits and reach their professional fulfillment through entrepreneurship. My personal purpose is to help entrepreneurs like you to become wealthy and to assist my Family Businesses, the 'Hotel Alternative,' which is expanding worldwide; you will benefit from the recognition of our chain of hotel alternative properties and my personal unbiased support.

The latest Travel Market Report this year showed that a staggering $17 billion, from the US alone, was spent by travelers in the first six months of 2012. American people decided that "enough is enough, there is no point in waiting to see what is happening next", locked their comfortable homes and went places, traveled the world. I don't know about you, but I love the American attitude and we have a lot to learn from their assertiveness. They choose places that have something different and a lot to offer. Luxury travel sales are booming and upscale travel is the new trend. With diminished drive and low self esteem generated by raising gas prices and unemployment, individuals across Atlantic, Europe and beyond are postponing travel plans each day. Our fear of spending could have a dramatic, immediate effect on potential economic growth and create a further financial 'locked-in syndrome' worldwide.

Statistics, however scary they may be sometimes, show us facts: cardholders are using their plastic cards and make the world go round! Fighting fire with fire, despite all odds, people start going places again, discover planet Earth, and even outer space. Richard Branson, who is my absolute hero, launched Virgin Galactic and lots of people would consider themselves very lucky when paying in excess of $200,000 for a suborbital space ride. Outer Space is his next territory to be flagged, and there is a long list of wonderful changes to our lives which were initiated by the very same generosity of Virgin's spirit which inspires Entrepreneurs like you and me.

Our noble mission may be insignificant but, right here, right now, on Planet Earth, thousands and thousands of families travelling away need a place which is private and comfortable and they can call it home.

The Hotel Alternative is a very intriguing concept and despite the fact that it is a labor intensive model, it brings a world of wonders to property owners and definitely doubles their income when compared with long term rentals. For most people, an investment property is the safety net for their retirement, or for unforeseen rainy days. It is important to maximize your rental income from day one and change the dynamics of your cash flow by taking control of your investment. To make your money go further, you need to get involved beyond the monetary aspects or delegate somebody you trust, to put your property on the hospitality map.

Travel and Hospitality are two industries joined at the hip, and they are driven by luxury travelers, some of whom are my clients and most of whom are to be yours. Families are trip planning again, and, multi-generation travel is back in fashion. Affluent travelers looking for "better and better" are happily spending on travel products but must be something new, something different. They want to have privacy and freedom during their trips, they don't want to be regarded as 'tourists' anymore, living in a suitcase in claustrophobic, exorbitant hotel rooms.

Travelers want to live like locals, have their own front door, their own residence! We are welcoming a new wave of savvy travelers, value-conscious when choosing accommodations, as they plan splurging on memorable outdoor experiences abroad, with their family.

Quality time, shared across three generation travelling together, is the 'must have' commodity and we are all craving for. It is in our nature to discover better things and there is a lot to choose from. We love to return to an old traditional family dinner, for some delicious 'home made' meal which only grandma knows the secret for, even when we are away from home. Under the same roof, old and young, we can bond together, sharing our old memories and enjoying quality time, in a home that is as nice and comfortable as our own, and we can call it 'home' for a fortnight.

The Market for The Hotel Alternative is a new but fast coming hospitality niche. Holiday Homes, Villas, Apartments and Cottages are saving millions to consumers, each year, worldwide. The savvy traveler will choose an apartment over a hotel room, and will rent a Vila for their relocation or choose a house to rent a house for their family reunion, if presented with the options.

The Hotel Alternative, Shakespeare Vila, Battersea, London

I.2. How can I help you double your rental income?

How to slalom throughout the upside downs of a recession? Challenging times are here to stay. I would like to invite you to take part in an innovative business model which was developed by myself and my two sons in response to, and driven by, consumer demand. I started my business by opening the door of my house to friends and family because I was a widow with three little kids and I could not travel in business style and live in hotel rooms, out of my suitcase. I returned to the old continent knowing that there are lots of people like myself, traveling with their families and they need a house, not a hotel room, a place that they can call it 'home' even for few days.

My journey was filled with hopes and disappointments and I have learned everything that I am sharing with you now, with the belief that what I do will bring quality into travelers' lives.

Hard work it was and ending my working hours with my head on the desk was somehow normal, but each returning customer brought me so much hope and wisdom, and sharing what I learned with people like you, makes it worthwhile. Above all, while trying to meet my guests' expectations, I managed to better myself and become the founder of a large community of property owners worldwide.

My business model offers a real home to thousands of people traveling with their families Away from Home. Looking at how our team of professional landlords is expanding globally, creating our own identity as The Hotel Alternative community, it is nothing more than the right response to consumers' demand. Imagine an exotic plant that has its organic needs to grow into a strong tree with flowers and fruits. Those fruits will provide the seeds needed for the tree to carry on a new species of successful hospitality. We create jobs, bring wealth to our local economy and motivate our families to carry on our legacy for success.

At first, my small businesses, which was "unheard of" or "unmet' was raising some, let's say, estates agents' eyebrows but that's all right, because, in their defense, this is a different business model, where everybody wins! Perhaps, just to be fair, I should mention that now, they are, lately, trying to do what we do! And, how would they know what is outside the estate agent's commission world?

As for my guests staying at our properties over the years, I am very grateful to all of them as they referred numerous friends as well as sophisticated corporate clients.
I went through some tough times but my strength always comes from believing that I can make a difference. Insignificant it may be, but what a great experience for our guests when they live like locals in a foreign country and have their own front door!

Where I am now, after all these years since I decided to create a new accommodation trend? I am travelling to your place, if you need me, to help you start your own Hotel Alternative.
I am going to travel, to meet property owners like you and me, so the world will have the chance to know them better, and travelers will stay at their places for a fraction of the price of a hotel room, and have their own front door during their stay. Personally, I can't bring myself to book a hotel room, so for my next trip I booked an apartment in Toronto, from a great girl, who is a professional landlady, a blogger, kind and smart, a person of many talents and her name is Kirsten. I am going to tell you all about her property in my next 'Away from Home' book, which is a guide for savvy travelers. Like me and you.

Where I am now? Hopefully, I am in your main contact list because I am ready to share with you my life time experience as a host, so you can develop your own hotel alternative business without wasting your time and energy on trying to figure out the small prints, as I did on my own.

I want you to focus on helping your family, bringing wealth to your town or village, and offering world travelers the unique hotel alternative experience at its best. The good thing about not giving up when times are tough is that, one day, by developing affordable, efficient services in innovative ways that meet consumers evolving expectations, your sacrifices will pay off. Personally, by not giving up, in very difficult times, gives me now access to more clients than I can accommodate at my own properties, and gives me the strength to help other people implement my business model and stimulate economic growth.

My business model is designed for you to achieve wealth and discover yourself as the truly strong minded person that you are. I will show you how, step by step, in real time. When can you start? All depends on you. There are immediate benefits to consider when running your property as The Hotel Alternative, and I would like to list just a few features which are defining a new formula for property investment:

1. Profitability: Renting your apartment on a daily or short term basis is more profitable than the traditional long stay rental and, it is, by far, the ideal rental model to maximize your income.
2. Flexibility: you can decide and control the period of time when you want to offer the service and, of course, you can have free use of your property for your own personal time.
3. Immediate confirmation of bookings (24/7) to avoid the possibility of overbooking;
4. Turn key Management tools: full details of bookings, availability dates etc. to save you time and to help maximize profits;
5. Confidence and transparency of information: from the property owner's administration site, you will have access to all information regarding bookings, dates and availability giving you total control of your property;
6. Optional Full Management for your property, my business model offers a personalized solution with a complete range of services including housekeeping and maintenance of your apartment, offered by our dedicated and loyal housekeeping team;
7. Keep your rental income from day one and do not wait for agents to forward your payment after weeks of waiting and commission deductions;
8. Enjoy your relationship with your guests and have no nuisance from licensed tenants;
9. Double or triple your rental revenue with no marketing costs with a formula which works even during difficult economic conditions where the demand for your Hotel Alternative is even higher;

I.3. Internet driven trends of consumers choice

Everything begins and ends with consumers' choice. When we start to understand consumers' trends, we know that we are going in the right direction.

Travel services seekers will respond to the new freedoms to develop their online search abilities. Who are they?

Internet users going online on the lookout for travel services, hospitality products, and everything else. According to latest statistics from The Internet Society, right now, there are 2,267,233,742 people online, which means that, actually, each third person alive on Earth is online, searching for something they need or they want. Information provided bellow by Internet World Stats, are relevant for us too.

WORLD INTERNET USAGE AND POPULATION STATISTICS						
World Regions	Population (2011 Est.)	Internet Users Dec. 31, 2000	Internet Users Latest Data	Penetration (% Population)	Growth 2000-2011	Users % of Table
Africa	1,037,524,058	4,514,400	**139,875,242**	13.5 %	2,988.4 %	6.2 %
Asia	3,879,740,877	114,304,000	**1,016,799,076**	26.2 %	789.6 %	44.8 %
Europe	816,426,346	105,096,093	**500,723,686**	61.3 %	376.4 %	22.1 %
Middle East	216,258,843	3,284,800	**77,020,995**	35.6 %	2,244.8 %	3.4 %
North America	347,394,870	108,096,800	**273,067,546**	78.6 %	152.6 %	12.0 %
Latin America / Carib.	597,283,165	18,068,919	**235,819,740**	39.5 %	1,205.1 %	10.4 %
Oceania / Australia	35,426,995	7,620,480	**23,927,457**	67.5 %	214.0 %	1.1 %
WORLD TOTAL	**6,930,055,154**	**360,985,492**	**2,267,233,742**	**32.7 %**	**528.1 %**	**100.0 %**

Ten years ago, everybody would go to their trusted local travel agent and take advice on where to go, think about it, think again, and maybe, go back to the travel agent to book their holiday. So what is happening now? Why are people choosing their products and making bookings online? Is it because we live in this 'Right Now Era'? Is it because The Internet is an open book for everyone, for absolutely everything and consumers are these new super humans with access to information? It is because we are aware that the costs for expensive printed brochures as well as the up keeping of the travel agents' shop are coming from our own holiday budget?

What makes travelers choose their accommodation in the spur of the moment and pay online? Before clicking on the "book now" button, accommodation seekers check out other people's reviews who offer unbiased advice based on their personal experience, they facebook, they tweet, they blog, and as a result they find our properties and save thousands for their travel trip, to be splurged on other attractions.

Everything that consumers are looking for constitutes trends. Personal experiences, our aspirations and our style of life, are the very fabric of who we are and confirm our status. Most of the time, travelers will look for **something special, different, cool, unique, luxurious, comfortable, private,** and most importantly, **decently priced**.

Home owners and Hospitality providers ourselves, we have to follow those trends because they generate demand for our product: The Hotel Alternative. Perhaps I should mention one of my clients from New Zeeland, Sandra, who told me that my property was a great home for her family and they could not believe how lucky they were to have such a great place during their trip. So, I asked what they were looking for, when choosing our place for accommodation instead of a hotel room. Sandra told me that her husband was searching on the Internet for **"best deal in town"**. Please, write it down, this is an actual trend! At first, Sandra didn't want to hear about going to a hotel alternative, as she thought there is something strange about having such a small price to pay for two weeks, for seven people. Comparing with local hotels, our rates were approx. 45% cheaper. However, when her son went online and found other people's reviews related to our properties, on Trip Advisor, they booked my house that day. Deep in her heart Sandra had that tiny voice inside wondering" what if' and 'how are we going to go to a total stranger's home and feel safe?!' Before they left home, she rang me and her anxiety was bursting from every single other question and I was thinking to offer her a free cancellation option, just to put her mind at ease. I told her that I do understand her concerns as a mother but they will have a real home and she needs to take that leap of faith for their own benefit. She realized that she was overreacting. When they finally arrived, Sandra was overwhelmed by joy and embarrassment but, now she is recommending us to so many clients, and she is one of our best promoters in New Zeeland!

How did they find us? They found us online while searching for best deal in town. How did they place their booking? They booked my house Online, after checking reviews from our previous guests. Sandra and her family are just one example, but, according to an Internet Research Company, more than 2.3 million UK net users logged on to travel sites in one week.

Why are internet users on the lookout for "best deal in town"? Why choosing a whole property instead of a hotel room is an exciting trend? Internet users are smart planning ahead and they are not only looking for value- for money accommodation, but they are seeking "better", privacy and quality. Travelers' living expectations during their trips are a tall order: they want their own front door, with more personalized space, more freedom, all wrapped up into the 'wow!' factor and luxury. As a result, new business structures, models and methods of operation come in, to meet consumers' expectations and follow internet driven trends of consumers' choice.

I.4. The 'Hotel Alternative': free ticket to serendipity

The global economic downturn is a strong reason for travelers to look out for 'best deal in town' and this trend will enhance your ability to head high towards profitability. 'Value-conscious' attitude is not a matter of 'limited budget' anymore, but a justified trend for big corporations, as well as rich people, sourcing for a deal and choosing well, as part of the Urban culture. Governments are desperately backing the fragile balance sheets of Financial Institutions but national debts are epidemics, and private households are the first victims edging out of the borrowing vice.

Most people will save for a year for their trips before placing a reservation. What this really means is that everybody, trust me on this, will Google, tweet, Facebook, blog, and weigh the options for their accommodation before making a decision. Impulse buy is a trend of the past. Austerity combined with Authenticity is a new style of life for most countries in months and years ahead, and travelers are not swapping their credit cards unless they are getting real value for their money.

With Governments increasing taxes aiming for 25% spending reduction, big corporations are reducing their budgets on travel and making drastic spending cuts and they are, also, "best deal" lovers. Out of all the allies fighting the war on borrowings, the United States is wisely not indulging in spending cuts, unlike European nations.

Economic Recovery needs sophisticated treatment and I do agree with the Americans who believe that “money goes round” policy topped up by an upbeat attitude could have healing powers and lead the way to long missed wealth.

Because it is 4th July 2012 today, I am putting pen on paper thinking of all travelers from the United States. I would like to say "Happy 4th July!" to all our guests staying with us in the past, at present and of course, in the future! We will keep our traditional "4th July" Special discount on, for all travelers from the U.S., each year.

What all governments should write on their wall is: “Back up the Airlines!” Denting airlines’ ability to flourish always had a drastic impact on inbound visitors and the number of visitors has declined by 30% since 2008. A new modus Vivendi is forcing people from all paths of life into a late retirement.

Keeping active into their late eighties, means that they will travel with their grandchildren and they will look for quality accommodation for their 'inter-generation family reunion'. Hotel rooms will not be their choice, but a luxury private home, yes, that will give them a chance to have quality time together, to experience the authenticity of real Italy, or Britain, or Canada and go back home with “forget me not” memories.

Family time needs privacy and flexibility which only a true home can offer. When it comes to privacy and sharing with your dearest and nearest, Hotels are too restrictive for family gatherings and business trips. Last decade is the best testimony for the 'Quality Time' trend, while the future few decades are definitely routed by the same signs: privacy, flexibility, luxury. All these measurable dimensions are Travel trends and I am looking out for more.

Share your experience as a landlord with me. Are people looking for that 'Extra', 'Better', or 'More' while travelling? Why not? We can offer them a whole house for the price of a hotel room! Are people looking for the Wow factor? Wow them! To achieve our customer's satisfaction, we have to open our minds towards a new modus operandi and offer them, in good faith, a free ticket to serendipity.

Welcome to The Harbourfront, Toronto

I.5. Differences that make the difference

What The Hotel Alternative does for you, the property owner?

The Hotel Alternative is created by home owners for home owners, and the real difference we can make in your life as a property owner is our unbiased assistance.

Since 2008 we live incredibly challenging, upside down economic times, and 2012 is the perfect time to become part of The Hotel Alternative community which is offering you a turn-key business model, at **no cost to you.**

Would you like to embark into an extraordinary discovery journey while your property is flagged on the Hospitality map and collect bookings while you are asleep? Would you like to know the **5 Key Features of my Turn Key Solution** for your rental property, best suited for property owners that want to double their rentals income? Here they come:

1. Allows you to focus on getting ready for occupancy and providing a home for your guests
2. Project Management guidance and support available 365 days a year, regardless your location
3. Calendar update and availability restricted to the Property Owner
4. Payments made instantly, by guest, at the time of booking, based on 'agreed by owner' rates
5. Sharing availability and accepting bookings as a chain of hotel alternative properties

Economic Change is a highly reactive element that readily forms successful methods with almost all other elements of our business life. Like Oxygen. The secret is to measure with precision the other elements first, and decide how much you will add, before mixing them. Real world becomes more competitive by the minute (or by the second for some of us), and when you have a good idea, you should, by all means, mix with others, learn from them, let them learn from you. Together you will create new methods, generate new reactions to achieve stability and eliminate economic turbulences for good. Are you thinking of Buying Options, Joint Venture, Syndicate Buying? Why not?! Invest your money, or other people's money, into property, but seal the deal with your time, your pride and care for your local community. Your new mindset will inspire and help the alienated property investor to enhance rental income and professional fulfillment through entrepreneurship. It is Decision time.

Join us and list your property live on www.thehotelalternative.co.uk

What The Hotel Alternative does for our guests?

In very simple words, I could say, The Hotel Alternative is **saving travelers' money while preserving the most important dimension of their lives: Quality**. This is exactly what we do for our clients. After all, every challenge creates an opportunity. The whole world is waking up to different truths lately, and, we all have to work harder to stay afloat and conquer life challenges. The Hotel Alternative will bring you wealth while saving $$$'s to your guests.

Reviews on Trip Advisor are live, genuinely written by travelers who stayed in our homes, having their own front door, living like true locals, while saving thousands for their stay. We benefit greatly from our guests' feedback because this is how we learn to be the best at what we do. Top properties will score 5 (out of 5) but scoring less, actually means that you should improve your services. Please reflect on my few tips on how to achieve 5 out of 5 from your paying guests.

1. Welcome guests with your heart of gold

Sharing your time with your paying guests at check-in, it is only fair. If you just think of how they made the trip to your house, at price, how very tired they must be after a long trip, and how much your warm welcome will help boost their confidence, it will make perfect sense for you to go the extra mile.

To let them wait for you to bring the keys, will dent their expectations of meeting their greeting host forever. Helping them bring their luggage inside your house is a very kind gesture and if you think that is too much, you are in the wrong business. When you agree on a time to meet and greet, be right on time. It is better to wait than be waited for by a group of tired people which are in the cold, outside your front door.

You can make arrangements for somebody you trust to welcome your guests if you are away yourself. A few minutes will be enough for briefing your guests on your property's guidelines and layout, sleeping arrangements, available gadgets; telling them about local shops and transport, nearest pub, tourist attractions and local events, will help them greatly. This is the right moment to shake hands and make friends for life. They will have their questions answered right from the beginning, and they will feel again in control of their trip.

2. Cleanliness and Maintenance

Providing a clean house is the holly grail of The Hotel Alternative, and a clean house is only clean enough if it is well maintained at all times.

You don't need to do the work yourself, if you don't enjoy labor intensive activities, even most people find them very rewarding, but you must supervise the people hired to help and be present to check their final touches. There should be plenty of availability for a good cleaning lady and a regular maintenance person in your local area or maybe a member of your family looking for part-time work.

I only wish I could employ all the wonderful people who offered to help me over the years and helped with no notice in my hour of need! I would not be talking to you right now, without their generous help! The Hotel Alternative would not exist without them and I would like to say THANK YOU from the bottom of my heart for their hard work and loyalty! As part of your team, their efforts will go a long way in achieving good feedback from your guests.

Expect guests to be grateful to them directly and tip them handsomely for providing such a remarkable clean, well maintained house. When you travel with your nearest and dearest, perfect hygiene and working appliances are a must-have- commodity. Just think of your guests as your own family!

3. Direct Communication

Communication, very simply, is what we tell other people, our message to be sent across, in our own words, or, what other people are telling us. The style of our messages could be direct or indirect for us to choose: speaking, writing, or...letting other people read our mind! I would always choose words, and if possible, put them in writing, and keep everybody in the loop.

There is nothing more frustrating for your client than not being able to communicate with you, during their stay. They should have a telephone number that is manned at all times, even outside office hours. If they only have your e-mail, it may not help when they are not inside the house, but in the street, trying to figure out how to get access.

There is nothing more frustrating for you than not being able to check if your guests are still arriving and when, as you are waiting for them at the property and perhaps, your guests can not activate their mobile phones yet. And, remember, your clients are from a different culture, most of the time. What works, then? Prior written communication does. Confirm everything in writing, give instructions for check in, directions to the property, and leave nothing at chance!

4. Listen with interest and smile

Your property is ready for occupancy, everything is immaculate and the smell of fresh coffee is inviting your guest to relax, they are all smitten with your place, so charming and boutique! Invite them with both arms to feel at home, encourage them to use all the little things you left for them, and point their attention towards your 'Welcome basket' or 'Hospitality tray'. If there is an Honesty Bar in the house, tell them how that works.

Now is the time to listen carefully to what your guests have to tell and give them the solution for their little problem, if any. Point them to the corner shop, where Jack, the owner, can provide fresh vegetables for them or drop fresh milk on their door step, in the morning.

Don't get upset, whatever their question might be, ever!

The question I suggest you ask yourself is: How would you like to go to a place where the person giving you the keys to a perfect place and showing you round, is surprisingly, dressed down, anxious and stressed? This is your moment of fame. Place a little white jock, be confident and friendly, but if you are too shy to shine, Smile! You are not on camera, true, but the power of your smile will take you a very long way!

Welcome to your London Home!

Welcome to your Toronto Home

Home owners' hot desk

II.1.When and where to invest

It is Decision time and you are ready to invest in your first property.

Is your property going to be Freehold or Leasehold?

When choosing a Freehold property, you accumulate not only wealth but power and control over your own asset and the land on which your property is build. You can develop the property further and most of your future property improvements will need no planning permission, or additional application to the local authorities.

You own the land and as long as you do not obstruct your neighbours from enjoying their own habitat, everybody lives in harmony. Complaints are in human nature and you could hear raised voices from unhappy neighbours, but all can be easily addressed. Make sure that rights of way are not blocked and disturbances rules are not ignored. You have your castle, and everybody else in your neighbourhood wants to live in peace.

When buying a leasehold property investment, have in mind that other residents will have a say because their interest as owner occupiers will be above yours, as an investor. You will share the use and the costs of communal parts of the building like the entrance, the court yard, the gym, or services provided to all residents by the Maintenance Company, concierge, lift, especially when your apartment is situated in a large development.

There are plenty of deals to have when a new development will start the building work for, let's say, for more than ten apartments. New buildings are unlikely to value up at present, unless the Developer is a household name and they have what they call 'in house' financial services and offer you a mortgage based on a valuation which is carried out by independent surveyors.

Times are difficult, new built properties will never value up unless they are decently priced, and because the surveyor instructed by your lender will take their comparable from the list of sold properties down the road, which are second hand properties, figures will not add up. The other buyers will be usually residents because the developer's price will have little margins for discounts, and property investors will not be attracted unless is a real bargain.

Think long term. With this in mind, when investing in a big development, unless you buy the Freehold property (lucky you!!!), your only option is a standard tenancy agreement and the Freeholder, the Management Company and the other residents will always have a say on who will reside at your property, to whom you are renting your property to and for how long. Are you buying/ leasing a property purely because the developer is giving you a good deal at the time?

Think long term. Ask yourself, if long term tenants will not be able to pay their monthly rent, what your back up plan is going to be. Ignoring your long term goals can shutter your investment, and your future developments. Having the option, I would not hesitate to choose the Freehold Boulevard instead of any other avenue. Whatever your options, be upbeat, go further, think, plan, act. It is never the right time for a passive approach.

Unless you commit yourself to a 'Hands On' policy, your investment is at risk. Passive investment is a myth. Self catering properties and The Hotel Alternative are key solutions for the savvy world traveler. With millions of travelers worldwide choosing The Hotel Alternative for spending quality time when away from home, you have millions of good reasons to take control of property investment and double your rental income.

Times are changing. Do you want solid grounds for your investment? Change is happening right now, and it is too chemically reactive to appear on our Economy without the photosynthetic action of Entrepreneurs. They are using their energy and determination to produce new concepts that would benefit everyone.
Change, like Oxygen, it is definitely in the air and constitute most of it.

II.2. How to choose your niche and rent right

First, you have to switch your mindset. When you invest your money into property, seal the deal with your time, your pride and care for your local community. There is a wealth of waterproof solutions and healthy alternatives to traditional real estate investment available to all of us. My business model was designed for people travelling Away From Home; it is a specific hospitality niche for Families, Executives and Groups seeking luxury accommodation. I am ready to share my fact findings as well as my client's data base with you. In any industry, learning new skills, takes time. If you want to make serious money from renting your property, you need to love people and be ready to apply the fastest and most effective way of maximizing your rentals income.

Renting your apartment on a daily or weekly basis is more profitable than standard long-term rental. Deciding on the length of your minimum stay will determine the volume of your bookings. Being flexible and accepting stays as little as two nights will attract higher rates, especially during off pick seasons. To attract great occupancy level throughout the year, consider lowering your rates for bookings which are longer than 28 nights.

Our aim is to provide high quality service to all guests, to ensure complete customer satisfaction, at all times. Our booking system provides immediate Confirmation of Bookings (24/7) to avoid any possibility of overbooking. There are more than 100 Management tools available for your use to make the booking process friendly.

You will have full access to details of bookings, availability calendar, events calendar, market trends, and property description, to save you time and to help maximize your profits. Our booking system offers both Confidence and Transparency of information.

From the property owner's administration page, accommodation seekers will have full access to all information regarding bookings, dates and availability giving you total control of your property and personal reservation system. We will assist every single step of the way with information on factors that affect your rental property: supply and demand, dynamic rates, affordance, market trends, and calendar of local events.

Sharing availability for relocation and groups throughout our chain of hotel alternative properties is the most powerful tool we have to eliminate vacancies, as we actively work to promote thousands of properties from the same platform: www.thehotelalternative.co.uk

II.3. Your property pays you

We all want to take a well deserved break, away from our daily routine and big cities or special places will come to mind. Except for the tag price of hotel rooms, not much would stop us travel the world. All airfare providers, big or small, are racing the contest to win our business, taking us places, by plain or train. Since we turned Michelangelo's dream into reality, there are no limits, we can travel anywhere in the world.

There is a rainbow of attractions and events all year round, which most people would love to travel to if they could afford the exorbitant hotel rates and your House could be the answer to accommodation seekers! When showing you why travelers will choose to rent your place, instead of the most extraordinary hotel room, you will love the concept! You will learn the secrets of how to double your rental income, 365 days a year, and how to welcome the world travelers to your house, help them feel at home and exceed their expectations. I will be next to you, helping you to create an exciting product: Your own Hotel Alternative.

As a big Thank You for buying my book, you will list your property, free of charge, on my website, www.thehotelalternative.co.uk whether your house to rent is an apartment in the city, or a remote cottage, anywhere in the whole world! **Listing your properties for free**, as a standalone bonus, will save you at least five figures marketing costs!

You have now the perfect platform for your properties, at your fingertips!

Reading my book you will gain instant access to unique techniques and trade tools, absolutely essential to your immediate success. Do you have a house for rent, anywhere in the world? I would love to help you double your rental income. Most investment properties will bring you wealth when let on short term basis.

Should you decide to rent your villa in the Alps, or your apartment in Toronto, or even your own home, while you are away, I am confidently opening the gates for you. Please step in now and add your own mark on the hospitality market. You will learn how to maximize your rental income in very simple steps, by the click of a button.

My business model on successful house rental was designed with you in mind, regardless where your home is located. What is happening next? I will assess your property first, and if I consider that our existing clients and prospective guests will benefit from staying at your place, I will start promoting your place and make sure that your Property pays you too!

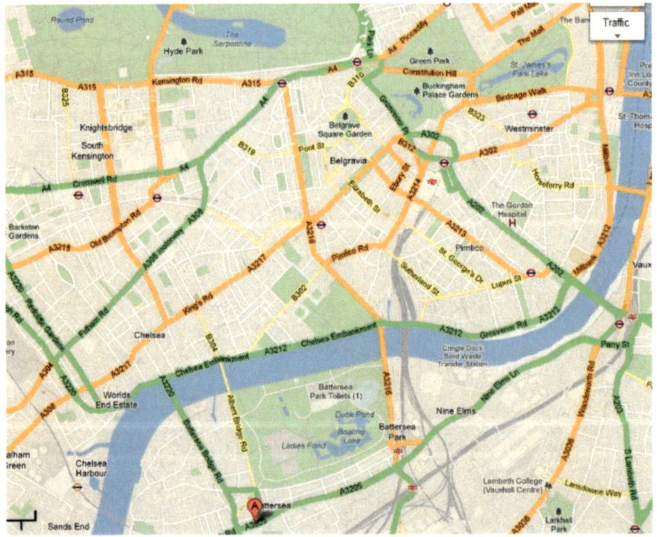

Relaxed and leafy, Battersea is one of the most loved villages in South West London

II.4. Knowing your market

When choosing your property, make sure that you put yourself into your clients' shoes. The property should be located near prestigious landmarks, parks, local shops and restaurants and have easy access to tourist attractions. Your local area should be busy and your property should be located within reach of most important places to be found in the whole of your city, or county.

When the neighbouring area of your property does not have the same level of prestige as the city area, it is very important to choose a good area in terms of entertainment!
A leafy district in a big metropolis will always be bursting with exciting events, shopping malls and attractions. As long as your property is part of a district with good transport links to the City centre investing in a leafy area will carry no risk.

In each country there are places of interest which have been neglected in the past, but they are part of a regeneration program or an upcoming area, where properties are still affordable. At any point you have to make sure that there are reliable transport modes available, so your guests will travel easily back and forth to tourist attractions.

Checking local Public records, is a worthwhile exercise as you will find out exactly what is happening, when and where. Each government will have developments plans published by the local council and this is where you should start your search. It is an exciting exercise and, please, do not hesitate to ask questions while there; make a note of all the answers to set the facts right and leave no room for confusion.
Keep your findings accurate and up-dated.

Perhaps, your own residential area is the best place to start investing because you know the local realities and how to overcome difficulties. You already have a taste of the local trends, annual events, your neighbours and local business owners. They will, all, help you if you ask them.

There will be plenty of mutual benefits as you property rental will attract more visitors and they will spend lots of money locally while residing at your home. The economic impact of tourist activities equals the revenue generated from persons who are visiting. Tourism is important for communities, and local businesses are benefiting from increased demand which generate more jobs and better living standards.

Tourism is considered to be a trillion dollar international industry. Latest statistics suggest an increase in travel spending and an upsurge in Consumer Confidence Index can be seen, as a result of financial health and spending power of the average consumer. Americans are family oriented and they love spending quality time at your hotel alternative. Canadians are spending just under 15 billion on their vacations in the US, one billion in England and just under a billion in France.

Your clients will be mainly professionals travelling with their families, couples or groups of friends looking for quality during they trips. Your guests are people to whom you already exchanged information, checked their details, their status and reasons of travel in your preliminary contacts. Your guests are not going to 'walk in' to make a booking; they will place their reservation well in advance. When you take their reservation you collect their ID via their credit card details, address, contact; e-mails and social media are helping you (and them) formulating a well informed opinion on who, where and what. After a while, your guests will be mostly repeat business or recommendations.

Where can you find a property that is well situated, for both your guests and yourself? You may be able to source a good deal for your property investment when a neighbour is moving home. A good location should keep your visitors busy from dawn until dusk, and keep your travelling time, to and from the property, to a minimum.

However, don't think that a rundown property situated in the very heart of the city will need no improvement and it will be an instant hit. It won't. At best, it will attract bad reviews. When your visitors are savvy enough to choose you as an alternative to hotels, they know what they want. Even more important than location is that your hotel alternative will offer your guests the comfort and amenities that they would expect from a hotel, but without the claustrophobic room size and exorbitant rates.

No Vacancies

Chapter 3

Pride and presentation

III.1. How to benefit from the world market trends

There is a well established trend for choosing a home instead of a hotel room for holiday, relocation plans, events or short business assignments. As a result, new business structures, models and methods of operation come in to meet consumers' expectations and follow internet driven trends of consumers' choice.

Before travelling, there are at least two big questions coming to mind. Staying at any hotel with your family means that you need few rooms. How are you going to balance the quality of your stay for six people, and how are you going to adapt your expectations to your bank account?

The hotel alternative provides an ideal solution for families travelling away from home and on the lookout for quality, privacy, comfort, authenticity and exclusivity. Not surprisingly, most travelers are excited by the novelty of the concept and loyal to their hosts with whom they created a bond during their stay, they go back to the same property.

I was very fortunate to have repeat business, people coming back to us and when we expanded our portfolio in the following year, we had plenty of bookings lined up. It is reassuring; to say the least, to have clients who are seeking our hospitality year after year, sometimes, few times a year. This is how we grow. We have to work very hard each time somebody stays with us, but as a result, our family business is expanding on demand.

In the last couple of years we found ourselves into a very interesting situation: we do not have enough properties for our own clients! With demand is so high, my main challenge is acquiring more property stock to cover essential repeat business.

III.2. Your 'Hotel Alternative' goes live!

Joining The Hotel Alternative community and activating your property to go live on our system could not be easier. Because we share our Front Desk with you, your job is basically half done. Assisting you from our end will free up your time and energy and allow you to focus on your hosting skills, checking in your clients and enjoying your life.

This is a great luxury which I did not have for myself but I am happy to provide it for you.

There are 3 Basic steps for your property to go live:

1. Describe your property, room by room, accurately
2. Provide a minimum 15 photos
3. Decide on nightly rates for or property be checking local trends

Once your property advert goes live, your routine is trailed over four modules:

1. Accept bookings
2. Check in your guests
3. Give support during their stay at your house
4. Check out your new friends and enjoy their comeback

Contact me with your questions. We are ready to give immediate kick start to your very own Hotel Alternative. The Knowhow of sustainable monthly rental income by trading within the International Hospitality Market, with no marketing costs to you, is at your fingertips! Optional, your rental home will be published in my book series 'Away From Home -The Hotel Alternative' to inspire, guide and help the Global Travel Market and its travelers.

Join The Hotel Alternative community now, and double your rentals income

www.thehotelalternative.co.uk

Please see an example of how to describe your property, to stand out from the crowd

"Byron Villa, two minutes walk from Albert Bridge and Battersea Park, London, Great Britain

Welcome to your home!
London accommodation doesn't need to be claustrophobic. Choose this entire property instead of a hotel room and you will have the benefit of large, well-lit and airy rooms throughout the house. From the moment you step inside, you will be wowed by the high

ceilings, splendid features and fittings which welcome you everywhere you go: living room, kitchen, bathroom, all three bedrooms.

From the window in the kitchen you can keep an eye on your children's play, while cooking dinner. When meals are ready you can gather round the dining table for a family dinner. Open up the doors to the living room, where you can watch TV or listen to your favorite music or read your book. It has been a long day and well deserved rest is awaiting you. Good quality beds, most of them versatile zip and link which could be kept together into a large matrimonial bed or as two separate, single beds, with luxurious mattresses and crispy linen will cushion a good night sleep.

But your home in London has more to offer: absolutely unique for most properties in the City, you will enjoy a large, vibrantly green private garden, with outdoor patio, comfortable

seating and sunny spots with wooden benches where you can read your morning paper or tweet, letting the world know what a smart choice you made when booking a whole house instead of a hotel room. For all I know, there is nothing better than a BBQ with family and friends during the summer time or a romantic candlelight's dinner, in your own garden.

The Spa-like bathroom also features a walk-in shower with wet area and bathtub.

After a good breakfast, you are ready to leave the house. Where to go?! There are myriads of options to discover the beauty of London: a stroll along Albert Bridge or Battersea Park will take you to Chelsea Embankment and Sloane Square, where you can rub shoulders with celebrities and Royals from all over the world.

Situated very conveniently in a safe, leafy area, our location offers local gastro-pubs with delicious food, coffee shop just cross the road, fresh fruit and flower market, and numerous reliable public transport links; there is a bus stop right outside your London property which will take you to London Victoria in ten minutes. Enjoy your stay in full and when you come back next time, you will be again, at home!"

III.3. Staging your home

Emotional comfort is what most people are craving for, when looking to discover new places, new experiences and get charged with new found energy.

No longer do consumers want to be like their neighbours and copy and paste somebody else's choices, they want to have something unique, better, different, more personal. When staging your property think how to surprise your visitors with your good instinct.

To connect emotionally your property in the city with your guests, technology could be a great catalyst for needs and wants: High speed internet, moods lighting, sound music system, flat screen televisions. If your property is in a remote location, you could replace technology with exotic amenities, spa, secret gardens, or woods. The ultimate destination for your guests is connecting emotionally with the surrounding environment, away from the usual buzz of a modern but hectic life.

Combining exclusivity with just enough technology, to create an aspirational style of living is a well-established trend of consumer choice. There are few landlords that went to the extreme length of energy and financial investment to achieve incredibly high spec, high end, up market interiors for their rental properties. There is a big demand for properties dotted with amenities and gadgets that are the latest on the market.

Don't think that your old faded furniture or radio will do. Install the latest music sound system, biggest TV, and, definitely, replace any avocado tiles, if any are left behind, right now. There is no room for compromises, and having the best you can afford, and more, for your paying guests, is a golden rule. My house is modest, but our rentals properties will 'wow' most people.

A friend of mine is buying run down places and transforms them into exquisite homes, reshaping old carcasses into fabulous living quarters. Even when the place is outside the main stream of attractions, he will spent every single penny on the latest, most sophisticated interior design features and, basically, bring Manhattan into the suburbs.

This Landlord is creating his own mark on the British property investment with an enthusiasm and determination that makes him a Lord of Vision. All his projects are the incredible result of progressive thinking and are built to last for the next few centuries. He knows that travelers are savvy, they are in the lookout for *unique*- authentic- exquisite, and aspire to reside at exclusive, trendy, expensive places, and they can have it, by a click of a button.

His latest project is an exclusive retreat, exquisite creation of brick and spirit in SW London. Set within a most sought-after area, this breathtaking seven bedroomed, seven bathroomed detached freehold property occupies an unique site nearby the former residence of President Dwight D. Eisenhower. Accessed via a private road, you will be welcomed by the grand entrance of the property and its beautiful gardens, garages and a separate annexe, as well as the main building itself.

Offering over 11,000sq ft of enhanced private space by the most refined taste in interior design, the whole house burst exceptionally high standards and specifications, throughout. Once you reached the threshold, the giant chandelier coming down from the top floor's ceiling is snowing its glamorous light far and beyond the marble spiral staircase, deep inside the very soul of the house. The well designed bright rooms are only matched by the wonderful entertaining space, cinema room, spa with swimming pool and wet rooms, outdoor kitchen, summer house, playgrounds which provide maximum privacy.

The ground floor comprises large reception rooms, dining room, conservatory, kitchen/breakfast room, music room, media room, office, utility areas with access to the basement and the outdoor space: garages and gardens. But there is even more to be mesmerized by: an outdoor kitchen on the decked area and a separate summer house for your family events and office parties, enhanced by inspiring natural colours at day time and outdoor lighting at night. Celebrating the beauty of this place would be reason enough for holding parties, year round.

As you discover the house, floor after floor, layer after layer, there is no end to luxury accommodation and amazing layouts designed to melt your moods in peaceful surroundings and total relaxation. In addition to the private bedrooms, you are drowned into further elegance and exquisite taste: meditation room, family rooms and additional pristine studio rooms, for the privacy of your overnight guests.

Situated in South-West London, only one mile from Wimbledon, Lothus Villa is located one mile from Wimbledon, within the Royal Borough of Kingston upon Thames which was the ancient market town where Saxon kings were crowned and is now a suburb a few miles South West of Charing Cross, eight minutes from Putney, and fifteen minutes from the myriad of shops at Westfield Shopping Centre. Wimbledon and Central Kingston are the main attractions of South West London, and it is connected to Twickenham, Richmond, and London Waterloo by National Rail trains and District Lane.

Shopping in Wimbledon is an exciting experience on its own, and when getting tired you could just try its dotted parade of bars and restaurants. The only Grand Slam tournament to be played on grass, Wimbledon is the favourite of many players and a highpoint of the tennis year, and only 11 minutes from the house (4 miles). Located within easy reach of The All England Lawn Tennis and Croquet Club in Wimbledon, for those staying in, outside the Wimbledon Tournament period, there is the huge, wild common on the edge of London, Wimbledon Common, famous for its Beetles, bridleways, windmills and rambling paths. Stag beetles, in particular, thrive in the bogs and well-established woods.

Most of the Common constitutes a Special Area of Conservation and Special Scientific Interest and spreads out over 1140 acres. Last vestige of the city, still shows ancients landmarks, and the old windmill dating from 1817, now a museum, marks the spot where Baden-Powell wrote part of 'Scouting for Boys'. Old English pubs are mushrooming around the edge of the Common, while Wimbledon Village with its famous gastro- pubs, rainbow of old and new shops alike, is just a short walk away. Whether you are strolling in search of outstanding natural beauty or for an elegant horse-ride, you are in for a great treat!

http://www.thehotelalternative.co.uk/Exclusive-7-Bedroom-Villa.html#.UDjJVt2PWvA

III.4. Go boutique: room by room

Think Boutique all the way! This trend for styling your interiors will work miracles for every single room of your property. A timid attempt to define correctly the Boutique phenomenon, will take us back to the 80's when London and New York opened their new catering niche of extraordinary facilities, design- driven rooms and excessive attention to customer detailed needs, from top to toe. Since then, the boutique concept not only went main stream around the world, but is part of what people want versus what people need, in terms of lodging and accommodation.

When dressing up your home and getting ready for occupancy, just think who is going to enjoy your boutique property, inspiring them to an aspiration style of life while they are away from home? Actually, better start thinking, who is NOT going to enjoy soft furnishing, intimate accessories, air-conditioning, mood lighting, small honesty bar by the extra large sofa, silk cushions and shire comfort written all over the place, under the magic of your music sound system, who can swing your moods from Earth to Heaven.

While you might think that styling your home could be expensive and out of reach for you, going Boutique, room by room, is nothing but a little bit of imagination going wild. Your 'Magic' tools and materials are easy to find and if use them with the right balance, nothing could go wrong: plenty of 'new vintage' mirrors, large framed photos or paintings, crispy linen and soft furnishings.

Start with reshaping the bedroom, where private means private, and even when travelling with your friends and family, privacy is not negotiable, intimacy is part of the 'feel good' factor. To enhance the moods between the four walls, you can simply dress the wall where the headboard sits, with floral or silk-like wall paper which matches the window dressing and the cushions. Made to measure Headboards are very expensive to purchase but if you buy a large piece of plywood from your local joinery workshop, lay some foam or a rich duvet and cover them with quality fabric, once placed on the wall, they will create an extraordinary central feature.

I helped my sons to manufacture incredible headboards, and while we were against the clock, it took us about 20-30 minutes for each headboard to be ready, go on the wall and change the room from nothing to something special. Michael utilized even the long strips of fabric remaining from the cutting to cover the bed frames and everything was, suddenly, touched by the magic: Voila!

I used smaller pieces of fabric, which were left over, to dress our existing pillows and top up the boutique looks of our already fabulous bedrooms, one by one. It will cost you less than £120 per room, if you buy the fabric from a local shop and do the work yourself. You can repeat the theme or change the color scheme throughout the house, and create individual looks for each bedroom.

Creating more sophisticated, dramatic looks for the matrimonial bedroom could be achieved with shades of black, silver, gray, or red. Going for lighter looks into the other bedrooms, will delight the children or grand parents. A few 'new vintage' mirrors and a few large paintings or framed photos will finish the boutique look throughout. I am definitely going to ask you to try, because it is not only a very rewarding experience for yourself, but a very flattering, new aspiration style, which will stay in your guests memories for a very long time.

Marketing: cocktail time

IV.1.Behind the scenes

Working with agents is a smart move because they are experienced, they know the inside out of their industry, they have the right connections, and this is their marked territory. Knowing which agents to work with is a total different story and takes years to find out.

In my experience, there are three different categories of agents, based on the way they get paid:

a. lead generation (advertisement paid upfront by landlord)

b. commission based model

c. booking fee paid by guest

When you pay a fee to advertise your property on a website, you will usually pay upfront, an annual 'one off fee'. This model is giving you direct access to your enquiries and depends on your speed to answer them and convert such enquiries into bookings. Conversation rate, in my experience, it is up to 1-2% and this is the reason I had to try all types of agencies available over the years.

After few years of loyal advertising with such website, you will have less and less enquiries, as they need to attract new business and to encourage them, the agent will offer 'feature property' to new comers. Of course, your advert will be pushed further and further down, and in no time, you will find yourself on page 32, if you do your homework (enough number of photos, abundant description, updates for your calendar daily, etc.).

While I do not have a problem with the home work, I do have a problem when I do not understand why my property falls down the listing, in a place where no one ever goes! Especially when you had results from the website in the past as you have been advertising for a decade and in your projections you, as a standard, expect that 2% of your booking will be generated from such websites. When the average time to view a page is less than 3 seconds, who is going to spent 96 seconds on the same website to find my property on page 32?

We have been told that updating our calendar more often will push the property up on the search and all properties adverts take turns to reach first pages, coming up as top results, weekly. However, we noticed that almost a hundred properties which were identical, provided by the same management agency, were coming up in top of the search constantly, keeping the first pages at ransom, without giving any other advertiser a chance to be, ever, on the first page, again.

I had to stop paying for an advert which doesn't stand a real chance to be read by anyone. Coming to think about, we paid just over £680.00 for the annual fee (this agent will not give a discount when you advertise just four properties; even you have been loyal for a decade!). We had absolutely no bookings, just less than 20 enquiries within the first 6 months. At that point, we realized that we lost a battle, but, hopefully, not the war. Back to the drawing board!

When you advertise on your agent's portal, on a commission based model, you signed an agreement with them (their agreement) and they are in full control of your calendar and rates, subject to their terms of business (usually small prints on few pages, written by a very smart legal team, to cover the agent's interest and it's relation with the customer but giving you no chance to protect your interest as a supplier). If things go wrong, and they do, you will be the guilty party. It is never going to be the agent's fault and the customer is always right.

Remember this because I learned all the lessons the hard way. Just to give you a tiny example, an agent called us and convinced us to accommodate a family which after a 12 hours flight, had no place to go, and their hotel was overbooked (nothing out of ordinary during the summer months in London, except 2012, when London become officially a 'ghost town'). Anyway, we agreed to accept the booking starting in two days time. On that very hot summer day, somehow, we worked out a miracle and furnished a 3 bedroom apartment for which we collected keys at noon, into a complete home in 6 hours, just to accommodate this family.

While we were running everywhere, the guests already arrived (two days early!) because the agent gave them the address without telling them that it is impossible to accommodate anyone on the same very day. It was a very nice family from Japan, on their first trip to London, and we took them to a local restaurant to have dinner, while we were still trying to figure out what are we going to do.

At first I thought it is an error, and I wanted to make sure these people are not going to be homeless after they paid the agency such a large amount of money. On their booking form was our address, all details accurate, except for the date, which was wrongly starting on that day, instead of starting in two days time. The agent's telephone number kept going to an operator in a call centre abroad, which was asking, very calmly, my credit card details,' spelling please', as if I was trying to make a booking.

I could not get hold of any of the people in charge from the agency who originally sweet talked me into accepting the booking in two days time. I gave them the address and explained that we will work throughout the night and "yes, we will have the apartment ready for occupancy in two days time, but not today". Anyway, we had to deal with the situation at our best ability as we were left with our hands full.

Because it was such a short notice, and the guests have been waiting for us to carry the furniture in, clean and so on, we said that we will not charge for the first night and would the agent agree with our price reduction and not charge their commission for the first night? What do you think they did? They charged us anyway and we never got anywhere on that refund. Remember, they were asking us for help and we went out of any comfort zone by 100 miles! Remember we worked tireless with our suppliers and hired more people to help us get the apartment ready for occupancy? How long will usually take you, or anyone, to furnish and accessorize an empty three bedroom apartment, two weeks?

There are no words to justify their behavior, just remorse on my side that I was so naïve to think that agents could care for anyone but themselves.

On different occasions, we faced similar situations, and we took the trouble to make room from our existing booking to accommodate other families which 'could be homeless' as the agents put it. In one occasion, the phone was ringing off the hook with the agent trying to convince us to take another booking.

Eventually, we discussed with our existing guests who were going away for the weekend and they kindly agreed to have people staying at the property while they were away. I was very pleased to confirm with the agency that not only that made arrangements to accommodate them but it will be free, courtesy of our existing guests being away from the property for that week end, and we will charge them only for the maid service.

Even we have been waiting for the guests, in good faith, until midnight, nobody showed up and from the moment I mentioned 'free of charge', we never heard from that agent ever, again.

In my records, these are just a few personal but sad experiences, filled with hazards with no end. Magic words on this subject: avoid 'One Way Street' agent agreements, whatever it takes.

c. Booking fees paid by guest

This is a relaxed model, when the agent brings in the business, gets paid his fee by the guest (for sourcing the property) and you take it from your door, without any interference from the agent. Their contribution is massive because they do all the marketing for you and have a drink on... somebody else, for a change! After years, I am still working with a few international agents on this model and I do learn from them, each day.

Their Customer Service is very efficient and they never stop to impress me. It is a mystery to me, personally, how they can charge the guest 30% for listing my property.
Again, working towards customer satisfaction is a complex process and requires team work from both landlord and agent but guarantees glorious time ahead for everybody.

I was very impressed by Local Nomad, a French company who reduced their fees when we reduced our rates to accommodate our guests' budget. Magic words: Win-Win-Win

What I learned:

When choosing an agent and getting nowhere fast, don't blame the agent; it's wasn't the agent's fault that you hired them in this new world of "Click now". It's never an agent's fault that you give away all of your control over your own property and happily signed all their paperwork. Is your mortgage going to get paid by itself?

Do not feel sorry for yourself, and do not blame anyone. It's not an agent's fault that a property owner signs an agency agreement giving the agent the power. It's not an agent's fault that a home owner (non- lawyer) signs a contract with an agent, with twenty full time lawyers ready to act against you.

And, definitely it is entirely to the home owners to notice that some agents stopped working for home owners and they are working for themselves, protecting their own interest, but that is normal.

I have to admit, it is beyond me to understand why people who survived the saga of buying a property, furnished it, putting their own mark and styling the property, people who are giving a soul to empty walls, would need an agent?

Perhaps the hard selling techniques do work and I experienced myself buying something I don't need. What stops you putting your property on the market yourself? What stop you from making money right now?

Let's analyze together a simple self assessment questionnaire:

1. Are you the property owner?
2. Is your property ready for occupancy?
3. Do you have 20 photos of your property available?
4. Have you been doing your figures and realised the opportunity to double your rental income with ease?
5. Can you to contact me?

If you answered 'Yes' to at least one of the above questions nothing will stop you to double your rental income, but yourself. The solution is to change your mindset, trust yourself and go out, in the World Wide Web!

www.TheHotelAlternative.co.uk

IV.2. Self-marketing and free platforms

21st Century consumers will expect to be provided with modern, high impact marketing content and materials, whether they are a regular advertisement in your local or regional press, billboards, video presentations at your local dentist Clinic, or on the back of your local transport /parking tickets.

Make sure your contact details are accurate and any phone number you choose as main contact is handled at all times, even outside office hours. Most of your last minute bookings will come to that phone number from people who have no place to go to, for one reason or another, and they will add the most valuable loyalty points for you, on the long run.

There are VOIP Systems (Voice Over Internet Protocol) which will allow you to divert your number to any mobile in the world and also give you access to a 'call log' service, to make sure you keep records for all calls. It is a very convenient service which gives you direct control over your communications, at very little cost. One day, we were told that we will have a different telephone number, with immediate effect and with absolutely no reason!

My heart start racing really fast, we were all in total shock, knowing that there will be people trying to reach us in the next hour and they will reach a dead line, they will try to e-mail us, and we will have no way of replying because we had no internet access! What a disaster! Took us eight weeks until we installed another line, but, as an immediate solution, Darie signed up with VOIP and he used his smart phone for internet connectivity, and we were live again, in 20 minutes. We checked in everybody that day, they never suspected we have been shut down for half an hour, but thanks to technology, life went on.

Do you want the rest of this story? Three weeks later and after forty eight hours and 28 minutes in total of actual calls to various premium numbers for 'Customer Service' from our previous provider , we were told that our number was requested by somebody else! I really thought that this is 21st Century and not some dark medieval age when "somebody" just takes what you thought was yours for a decade.

All I hope is that you have now the magic words for connectivity: Go VOIP.

Coming back to your marketing campaign (I could not help but share our dreadful experience that lead us to use our telephone system, just in case, similar hazards could struck), all particulars you will insert in your professionally designed advert, regardless how basic or sophisticated, are crucial, invaluable tools. Make sure that your e-mail goes to your smart phone and that you answer all messages wherever you are in the world. Any marketing campaign you will initiate, should reach the widest target audience possible.

As a progressive 21st Century landlord, it is vital to refresh all your communications collateral providing clients with modern, effective contact channels, so your high impact marketing materials will effectively sell your property. Social Media is becoming an increasingly important source of communication with your customers and for interaction between customers, and your campaign would definitely benefit. When promoting a bespoke product you should have a bespoke attitude, your tweets or status updates on facebook should be specifically tailored to both your property, from one hand, and your guests' time frame and profile, from the other hand.

IV.3. Your property on the map

Considering your target audience, your marketing strategy should be a cocktail of traditional tools (such as letters and canvassing) to raise immediate local awareness for corporate interest and social media networking. Ultimately, all efforts, big or small, will pay off, and I can guarantee that as a member of The Hotel Alternative community, you will have the best kick start you could ever imagine, with a personalized high-profile online campaign, that will put your property on the hospitality map.

Our standard revised marketing package available, FREE OF CHARGE, to all landlords' members of The Hotel Alternative community will include well tested practice to capture a global audience:

1. Listing your property on our property portals: www.thehotelalternative.co.uk for international properties and www.luxreslondon.com for London properties, with direct synchronized calendar to our distribution channels worldwide
2. A feature internet campaign through 'BEST DEAL IN TOWN' series
3. Listing on social media sites including Twitter and Facebook
4. A local canvassing campaign as part of 'Open house' launch
5. A full listing with photos on all major international property portal displays
6. A Google AdWords campaign as part of The Hotel Alternative community
7. A highly visible presence on our regular email marketing and Loyalty Voucher Program
8. Editorial, showcase interviews and blogs advertising throughout traditional and Social Media
9. Newsletters, press release, TV, Radio in associated campaigns with our partners
10. Published showcase in book series "Away From Home- Best Deal in Town" for each Edition (depending on your property geographical location)*

**Please note that for request of Professional photography and drawn floor plans to highlight the best features of your property, a small professional fee may apply to strictly cover our production costs.*

IV.4. The real cost of bookings (fees you should not pay)

Some agencies call themselves "home owners- friendly" and this is true to some extent. You pay for the advert in advance, usually for the whole year but nobody will tell you anything about "what if situations" and I had few experiences myself, which could cloud anyone's mind with anger and frustration. When paying a set fee, you will go for the cheapest option; just to see how it is going to work.

For listing your property without photos you will pay just over £200.00 and you will see a few timid enquiries and no bookings. After four months of no results, I went back to question the adverts features, which was not working and wasn't cheap at all after all. The sale person at the other end of the phone explained that it was my choice to have a very basic advert and, tempt me into up-grading. From my own experience, upgrading did not work either.

A sale person is paid on commission and they will advise you to buy extra features and up-grade to a 'Feature Property' or up-grade to gain exposure to a different country, or up-grade for translation in a different language, and so on. You will be paying well above your original budget, perhaps 4 times more. The real benefit will not show for a while, and we all could appreciate why, and accept the fact.

However, your patience could come to a halt when you will discover that because the agency listed other 50 identical properties from a big apartment supplier who runs a block of flats, and your feature advert will never come up on the first page, as promised. Your advert will not be found by people looking for a property like yours simply because your 'Property Feature' is on page 32! All they will see in their 3 seconds surfing on that agency website will be pages and pages of the same property, or collection of properties from the same owner and not various properties from different home owners.

The Hotel Alternative- advertising features

As property owners ourselves, we are aware that featuring your advert efficiently is crucial to your property exposure, to your level of occupancy and ultimately to your cash flow. Listing with www.thehotelalternative.co.uk as a member of The Hotel Alternative community is, at present, FREE OF CHARGE and includes attractive features.

Depending of your advert being promoted with our live online booking feature, you will see instant results. Should you decide to have enquiries placed first, before accepting a booking it will discount your level of bookings quite dramatically because visitors are placing their reservation online, instantly, without placing an enquiry.

To make it possible, we are working tirelessly on constantly improving our main advertising features, which are listed below:

1. Exposure on international sites from The Hotel Alternative account: Global Distribution Travel and well established sites like Flip key, Holiday Lettings, House Trip, Local Nomad, Loving Apartments, Vacation Rental, Home Away
2. Full description page of your property which you can edit at any point once the advert is live
3. Upload up to 24 photos
4. Availability calendar accurately up-dated with each new booking or change
5. Customer and property reviews
6. Exposure on www.thehotelalternative.co.uk and all our partners' websites.
   We will take your The Hotel Alternative advert information and build an advert for you on all our distribution channels. We will use a minimum of 15-20 Photos to case show your property
7. Synchronised availability calendar

Any changes you make to your The Hotel Alternative advert will be updated on all your adverts from your unique The Hotel Alternative account.

I believe that to achieve similar exposure with what The Hotel Alternative offers you free of charge, on a spectrum of only 10 holiday websites, you will need a budget of £ 5,000 per property, just to start you off. Should you decide to advertize separately with various website would normally cost you from £238.00 for a basic listing (with no photos) to Upgrade products which start from £379.00- £680.00

To avoid the nightmare of double bookings, as you will need to update your availability calendar for each site, each time you receive a reservation, it is virtually impossible. To find the right system and hire a professional distribution channel manager, you should allow further costs, which will total, easily, £25,000 per year. Your business will generate enough for you to support the infrastructure but you should consider getting all, as a turned key system available to you, now, free of charge.

If you have any questions or need any help, please do let me know. I like sharing. Should you have advanced knowledge on these subjects, please contact me.
I love learning from somebody who knows more, and 'knowing for knowing' is my new found freedom.

IV.5. 'Five a day' Versus the vacancy syndrome

Socialising with your customers is all about your online presence and making other internet users (over two billion) aware of what you have to offer, both spiritually and commercially. Of course, this is not the right place for a philosophical essay, but even the most spiritual people need material things, logistics, accommoation, transport, food.
Is it now a virtual world and so we prefer to stay connected with raither than our own immediate reality, or can none of them can exist without the other one anymore?

Pehaps,the answer is not an easy one and requires sophisticated honesty, especially when we go down the route of consumer demand and trends. Most definitelly, social media and social networking are keeping the world going round.Our evolution will be helped or killed by technological progress. Our destiny is in our own hands and right now we can enjoy a wide spectrum of choices.

Social media and social networking are part of the same organic medicine: "Five a day" to avoid surgery at later stage. I know home owners who really struggled before but once they start taking their "five a day" they cured their vacancy syndrome. My recipe is very simple: take five daily from of the 'vitamins' listed under social media and social networking, and it wil work wonders.

Twitter is my favorite because is so short and sweet, easy, relaxed method of communication, almost like opening a window for fresh air. There are Twitter Networks, direct message (DM) to another Twitter user, TwitPic, links and we can use them with only one rule: 140 carachters.

Your professional diary could be published instantly, online but it is called 'Blog' and it is a very powerful tool and I did not realize how fast news can travel these days. My blog on Chelsea Flower Show could be a good example, most people who read it, found it useful and inspiring. Few months later, my excitement was well understood, even at the time, some found it too emotional.

***

"Chelsea Flower Show- Mecca of blooms and Celebrities

We are just a few days away from the most exciting few months of the last sixty years, British Summer 2012- the celebration of The Diamond Jubilee. While May is still spoiling us with glorious days, splendid recent memories from Chelsea Flower Show are bringing a smile on my face.

On its 99th year since first founded by Sir Christopher Wren (1682-1692), this year's event was an absolute bliss, an extraordinary journey of mind and spirit, brought in by the eight hundred exhibitors who lashed their creative genius over eleven acre site at Chelsea's Royal Hospital Gardens and transformed it into a Mecca of blooms and celebrities.

We have been proudly accommodating few of the show's exhibitors during their stay in London, for almost a decade. Trilled with anticipation, I keep an eye on their future plans. Also, I may get some tips for my garden, as I don't really know how to keep my plants alive with the Hosepipe Ban's new regulations of this year. Hopefully, next year we will have more rain and I will learn a few gardening secrets from them and I will not feel so embarrassed when they come again! Luckily I found a new garden centre near my house, which will help my limited budget!

Year after year, the standards are raised incredibly high, and not sure what more we can witness next year, when we will celebrate a century of Flower Extravaganza. Ever inspired by artistic trends, words are not enough to describe the aphrodisiac cocktail of sophisticated smells, colors, vision and energy at this year's event.

Apart from the wave of tourists and visitors that overwhelmed us with joy during the show and transformed London into an exquisite vibrant place, there is a certain air of celebration and love which makes life worth living. People are happier, drivers are more patient, but above all, a mark of pride of being local, is obvious on everybody's faces.

My guess is that when June will knock on our doors, we will finally understand what being Great is all about and should anyone tell me that they don't care, I will not believe them (by the way, this is another local trend but it will be gone forever once the Olympic Games will start, because everyone will be part of the Greatest event on Earth!).

Being a Londoner it is the greatest feeling I have ever experience in my entire life, and unless you have to earn the privilege, it is easy overlooked. Just witnessing the rainbow of events raining on us this summer makes me recognize even more what a Great nation we are. Great Britain leads the world through the power of art and spirit, and taking part, even in a very insignificant way, it is a privilege second to none."

27th May 2012, London

***

I have to mention Facebook, but not sure where to start or what to say, because it is bigger than life itself, and, personally, I do not use it. There is nothing about Facebook you don't know and because I have so much fun with Twitter I will keep my loyalties with my followers, for now. Any child will tell you "how to facebook" but, if I look at statistics, I can see that you are there already!

Twitting from dawn till dusk

Renting your home through professional channels

V.1.Relocation clients living at your property

For people relocating to another town or country, exclusivity is not a luxury but a necessity. With personal experience in international relocation, we provide tailored solutions to our clients seeking a home away from home for themselves and their family. We are experts in looking after people and our focus is set completely on our guest's individual needs, and specific circumstances during their temporary accommodation. Being a 'pet friendly' landlord would make a big difference.

Our customer satisfaction drive is founded on real time support generously offered by our growing team of home owners. The needs of a family relocated at your property will revolve round practicality and basic inventory for your property, rather than 'wants'.

Because relocation is a well-planned form of travel, it will not be left at chance nor will be looked at in the last minute. Perhaps, there are relocation agents acting on their clients' behalf, or, maybe, the company, if it is large enough, pays for relocation of new employees and has a special department taking care of their accommodation needs. They will always place their reservation well in advance, they do not cancel them, and if anything will change from their requirements, could only be their departure date, when they need to extend their stay.

Relocation is an ideal source because it provides Advance Bookings which will raise occupancy level and give your cash flow a welcomed bust. There are agencies bringing in the guests for you early, but paying you late. You need to be firm about your rules and request the payment up front. An agency will charge their client in full at the time of their booking but they will only pay you 48 hours after the guest checked in.

***

Tips for preparing your property room by room

Kitchen

You already know that a fully equipped kitchen will fill your holidaymaker heart with joy and happiness. They may choose to use it or not, but it is there for them if need it. When we have a family who is relocated to a different country, they will stay with you for few months continuously and you should consider providing them extra items for their use, to help a stress-free stay. This extra attention to details will increase the chance of an extended stay or repeat booking.

You should not leave anything at chance and with all good intentions, provide a copy of the inventory and leave it in a drawer in the kitchen. Ask your guests to add more items to your list, should they need something more special for their stay that you did not consider yet. This will be a delicate way of asking for their permission to understand better their style of life and keep records of your inventory without offending them.

In the kitchen should be enough quality crockery and cutlery for your maximum occupancy, replacements for breakages and additional items for extra visitors

Bedrooms

Keep your options open and invest in twin beds as they are very versatile and could be used either as a large matrimonial bed, or as two single beds. You can ask in advance and instruct your housekeeper which way to prepare the beds, as you need different type of sheets when you split the twin bed. There will be a box with extra blankets and pillows for each bedroom.

Essentials

Most definitely, everything should start with your Hospitality Tray: biscuits, tea and coffee, sugar, and salt and pepper. Essential items like First aid kit, Travel plug adaptors, iPod docking station and Universal phone charger, there are details which you can think of in advance; when tired guests who just arrived after a long flight, can find such items for immediate, urgent use, you are a perfect host.

A good host will definitely have an Essentials' checklist for every single new reservation, and especially for the relocation clients: Kitchen roll, Washing up liquid, Dish cloths, sponges, Matches, Toilet roll, Bin liners, Spare light bulbs, Washing liquid, Hand soap, Broom, dustpan and brush, Spare batteries, few books, DVD's, children games to keep them busy while their parents have their hands full with unpacking or having a coffee

***

For more advice and new ideas

please e-mail me

Marina@AwayFromHome-book.com

V.2. Holiday makers and what they expect

Most seasoned travelers are loyal to their hosts and go back to the same property. I was very surprised to see repeat business coming back to us even when we had moved to a different property in the following year. It is reassuring to say the least, to have clients who are seeking our hospitality year after year, sometimes, a few times a year. This is how we grow. We have to work very hard for every single penny, and our performance is only as good as our last review but our family business is expanding on demand.

I cannot thank enough to all our guests for crossing the threshold of our homes with an open mind and noticing how much good heart there is in everything we do. Thank you!

Never treat seasoned travelers lightly, thinking that they only come during the summer or once a year. When they like your service, bringing their business travel to you, will be just a natural choice. We are treating all our guests with the utmost care and welcome them in our houses with same joy. It is the seasoned travelers who introduce us to their friends, to their work colleagues or to their relocation plans.

To request your loyalty voucher
please e-mail me
Marina@AwayFromHome-book.com

V.3. Needs and wants

Our properties are a smart solution for people travelling with their family, groups of friends and corporate relocation. What about, famous people? Do they, also, choose our properties over hotel rooms? Absolutely yes! If only I could have enough for them!
What about rich people? Do they need us too? Of course, they do. They are not our target audience, but, we accommodate them as well. Movie producers and their teams, Royal Family members from abroad, visiting our country, Hollywood House names as well as hedge fund managers or private banks executives.

The message we are sending is “Welcome to your home!” and our story development relates to the special nature of customers experience, location and exclusivity, affinity group travel and how clients- to- be can identify themselves with our product. Our accommodation model is in demand because of two main reasons: Quality and Privacy.

The economics are favorable to all type of clients and the Boutique phenomenon goes up a notch or two, who is going to complain? A house, when styled in a boutique fashion, will gain a quick reputation and bring regular repeat business, and it will be no financial volatility or profitability drops, even in the most challenging economic times. To remain competitive and desirable, we have to adapt our properties to the changing needs and wants, to embrace our customers’ preferences, expectations and demands.

Looking at the needs of individuals, we should consider all basics and cover all grounds.

There is a newly form interest for The Hotel Alternative from a niche customers who are in their early 20s to mid-50s, with mid- to upper-income averages from small groups of friends, to Families with one child, and they all want more than they need.

They are focusing on style and distinction while designing their image as successful individuals. They are looking for differentiated property able to fulfill their individual needs for warmth and intimacy.

Our travelers expect more than simply to fulfill their needs like comfort, convenience, security. Status stories are the reason behind a relentless acceleration and amplification of their wants: cool information, excitement, undivided attention, helping raise their personal manifestations of status. They are looking for quality in your property but their 'wants' are becoming a form of acquiring status, more than anything else, and if we could help, we will deliver the 'wants' in top of their needs. Acquiring 'story status' while living temporary at an exclusive property could help them and, I understand from one of our regular clients, that it is a lot easier to boost your image by renting an extravagant place than acquiring status by eco-credentials or non-profit activities, but I do not subscribe to the theory that this is a form of social manipulation.

Whatever our clients' motivations, their 'wants' are just another notch higher within our panel of standards and not a real challenge, considering they are paying for.

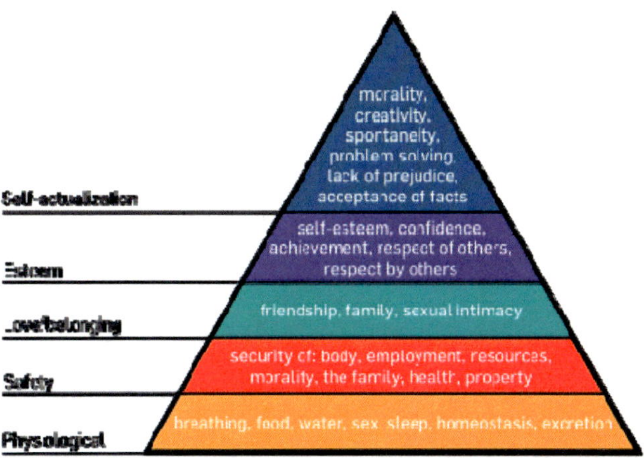

Apparently, Maslow's hierarchy of needs shows the pattern for human motivations and it is represented by a pyramid, starting with more basic needs at the bottom and evolving to the top. I remember that one of our clients was the hero of a local restaurant as he kept them busy overnight, for two weeks in a row, during their stay with us, and the restaurant made a fortune in tips alone. I introduced the place to my wealthy clients and I have lunch there sometimes, because the food is absolutely incredible; each time, the owner of the restaurant is asking if they are going to return anytime soon…I met extraordinary people and managed to deliver them what they expected from The Hotel Alternative, but there are efforts to be made in order to meet and deliver their expectations. With only one exception, which I am not going to mention here, people staying with us are very kind, they do appreciate our efforts to create a place that they can call it 'home' and when money is no object, no effort is too much for their 'wants'.

***

Welcome to my street: 'Revenue Avenue'

VI.1. Sharing availability as a chain of hotel alternative properties

Based on the 'Knowing for knowing' principle The Hotel Alternative is offering you complete unbiased guidance, and I will show you how to achieve financial freedom from renting your property, in 7 modules:

1. Sourcing your investment property and ground work assistance

2. Staging your home and getting ready for occupancy

3. Creating your Front Desk to control your calendar and rates

5. Launching your property live

6. Getting connected to our booking system

7. Put your property on the trusted Global Hospitality map

We are creating a major network of online travel distribution and our ever growing Global affiliate program needs you. Based on good reviews which are shared online, by our existing guests, our successful model is overflowing by repeat business. With more and more property owners joining us worldwide, we are out there in the World Wide Web, inviting people to our homes, knowing that they will have a wonderful, unique experience living like locals, having keys to their own front door, while Away From Home.

People seeking alternative hotel accommodation, do check for availability and after reading others reviews shared by previous guests staying with us in the past, are confident in placing their booking online! Your Property will be bookable online or by e-mail request, you choose the right method for yourself, but hundreds of thousands of affiliate sites, will work on promoting your property live.

Have you been advertising already with other websites? Our Channel Management Solution allows you to update third-party extranet calendar, with which you might have direct contracts, eliminating the off chance of double bookings and time-consuming updates. Our booking system requires no training, or software installation on your local computers.

What you will achieve once you enter my street 'Revenue Avenue'? Except for the fun and confidence you are going to experience in this journey, there are 12 major milestones to reach, one by one:

1. Make money in a rising or falling property market
2. Master your skills into Confidence and cash in immediate benefits
3. Take part in an exciting and sophisticated market trend expanding on demand, worldwide: The Hotel Alternative
4. Access free marketing platforms and portals to reach thousands of travelers instantly from one place: your virtual Front Desk
5. Bring your own mark in assisting our niche: Relocation, Holiday and Corporate market
6. Benefit from the most powerful marketing strategies with the click of a button
7. Create Wealth for yourself and attract wealthy travelers to your local community
8. Learn the entrepreneurs' best kept secrets for guaranteed success
9. Measure your Strengths to eliminate your Weaknesses
10. Create your own The Hotel Alternative and gain your financial freedom
11. Plan your Succession Management
12. Share what you learned with likeminded people in your community and pass on Your Legacy for Success

***

VI.2. Enquiries, attractive rates and unique features

The pick of your enquiries and bookings will match the dates when there is something new happening locally. Changing your standard rates could help you achieve a very good year yield. Our booking system provides a feature called 'Day of Week pricing' which enables you to change the prices, for minimum stays or last minute deals, instantly.

Applying discounts and special offers for festivals, religious events like Easter and Christmas, or cultural temporary events and exhibitions will make your property very attractive and popular. For the low seasons, make your 'best deal in town' ideal for any budget because the right price will potentially keep your property fully booked all year round.

Personally, I will not bank on major international events, like the Olympic Games or Royal Weddings, because regular visitors will avoid crowded places, and they will go anywhere else but where extra millions are gathering, whatever the reason. The summer of 2012 was a disaster for all accommodation providers in London, while nearby European location reached the highest level of occupancy in the last 50 years.

I went to Rome during the Olympic Games to see what was happening and to my surprise, everything was overpriced, over rated, with very disappointing standards, but fully booked.

In London, there is a big hotel chain going out of business as a result. Lots of professional landlords had to drop their rates below the breakeven point, and, keep properties vacant across London's main boroughs, with level of occupancy going well below 20%. Media was sending all the wrong signals for more than a year, gossiping on how bad and dangerous London is going to be, officials were sending their 'warnings' and locals left while visitors did not come.

Consequences: restaurants in Central London were absolutely empty, Sloane Square Tube Station was deserted on Monday mornings and major shopping streets famous for their retail attractions were abandoned. I had Kings Street in Chelsea, all to myself, and I did not like it. Officially, London was a 'ghost' town during the Olympic Games.

So, why, did everyone avoid London? People panicked, they were afraid of mayhem and did not enter London. There was absolutely no hazard, billions of people witnessed the greatest celebration of sports of all times, and we will be mesmerized for decades to come by the army of unknown volunteers , thousands of athletes, and the powerful minds behind the scene who provided out of this world logistic solutions. The only client who did not change their plans and travel to Paris or Rome this summer, was the company who provided the genial logistic for the Games!

***

VI.3. Bookings, confidence and transparency

Bookings are the result of decisions made by well informed people who trust our product. There are two major dimensions which will influence a good decision: confidence and transparency. Who are our clients and why do they place bookings with us? Our bookings are coming from:

Relocation channels

Government Bodies

Events and logistic companies

Banks and insurance companies

Religious groups and churches

Universities and International Schools

Seasonal Holiday Seekers

Sport clubs and International Sport Events

Art and Entertainment Festivals

Media and Advertising companies

Film Industry

When a reservation is made for business purposes, the person placing the reservation will provide not only their selected dates but a list of specific requirements and if they don't, you should ask: how many single and how many double beds, how many bathrooms, etc. All communications must be very clear and I always ask the client to confirm by return my e-mail listing their requirements placed over the phone.

Even corporate guests could place their booking online like everybody else, but they don't and you should offer your assistance and give them the option to make payments using other secure payment methods that suits them best. All fees for extra beds or chargeable services should be stated very clearly.

Being transparent and fair is the only way you can influence the level of confidence of your client. Without transparency or confidence, there are no bookings. After a booking is placed and payment is collected, make an effort and liaise with the management company regarding guest arrivals and departures and make everything effortless for the event organisers, as they have their hands full at all times and they will appreciate you going to extra mile.

Why thousands of families, couples, executives and groups choosing The Hotel Alternative over hotel rooms is very easy to understand. Asking your guests to express their immediate thoughts to define their own experience staying at The Hotel Alternative, in less than 10 words, could help you figure out what makes them coming back. Please have a look at what our guests think about our houses:

***

"House to suit all needs – even for old and grumpy" Audrey, Australia

"Whole house for a fraction of a hotel price" Scott, UK

"Best option for business stays; only advantages", Mike, US

"Truly a home for our family" Sonia, Italy

"Doesn't get better than this, big house, next to a big park, perfect!" Dan, Ireland

"Independence and comfort for a more enjoyable stay" Debra, Canada

"This really was better than my own home!" William, Germany

"Tailor made services to suit all our needs" New Zeeland

"Like our Home but with fully equipped kitchen and Professional staff!"

"Central and safe location, in leafy residential district, true home"

"Comfortable and spacious to suit our needs"

"Great place for our big Family to gather together"

"Happy parents from Australia visiting their adult kids in London"

***

Also, our guests found very useful additional detailed information on the local area and local transport.

***

Additional Location Information

Battersea is a leafy and well to do suburb of South London. Home to a population of mainly young professional, it has seen a revival of its popularity in the past couple of years with myriad of terraced coffee shops and dining establishments' springing up everywhere within its borders. The quiet and leafy streets are bathed with sunshine during the summer months and you can regularly see the locals jogging and riding bikes through the narrow streets

We have compiled this short guide of the top spots within this diverse and beautiful part of London to make sure our guests can make the most out of the local area.

Battersea Park

Battersea Park is one of the main public parks in London. Whilst it doesn't enjoy the popularity of Hyde Park or Regents Park, many consider it to be a hidden gem and a far more enjoyable place to spend an afternoon. Battersea Park is most notably known for its leafy pathways, splendid gardens and chilled out atmosphere. Take a stroll through the 198 acres of green spaces and you will be greeted by dog walkers, families and fitness fanatics out to enjoy the sunshine. You will also discover a lake where you can rent pedals, a restaurant, plenty of sporting facilities and even a children's zoo.

Battersea Park is also home to many events usually held at the Battersea Evolutions; an extremely dynamic dinning and events arena. From rare antiques fairs to arts exhibitions (at the Pump House Gallery) and even steam powered fun fairs, Battersea Park is always offering something to captivate its visitors.

Prince Albert Pub: located by the Albert Gate at the west end of the park, offers great food and a perfect place to enjoy that traditional English pint.

Albert Bridge: famous for its gothic design and the lights that illuminate it at night (a good place for those memorable holiday photos).

Chelsea & Sloane Square

Chelsea is the birth place of many youth cultural revolutions, the "swinging 60's" started right here on King's Road, as did the punk movement of the 70's. Today Chelsea remains the fashion Mecca of the Capital with exclusive fashion boutiques peppered from the west of King's Road all the way to Sloane Square / Sloane Street and Knightsbridge (For Harrods).

Chelsea is located just north of Battersea, to get there from our apartments is both quick and easy, either grab the 44 bus from outside the property, going towards Victoria and disembark at Sloane Square. You can also walk to Chelsea, simply follow Albert Bridge Road, cross the river ad continue straight on. Walking takes about 20 minutes.

Sloane Square also has an underground station, on the Circle and District Lines.

Chelsea and its neighbour Kensington are also the home to some of the most famous museums in the World, including The Natural History Museum and the Victoria & Albert Museums - Proving that Chelsea is not only a Mecca of fashion but also one of culture and science.

Clapham Junction

Clapham Junction is most notably known for its high street and popular bars. From department stores to boutique health shops, the high street has plenty to offer. Here you will also find Jamie Oliver's restaurant and shop, Debenhams department store, a myriad of shops, hairdressers, restaurants' and bars. To get here couldn't be easier, from the bus stop located 20 meters from the property take 344 towards Clapham Junction. The journey takes less than 5 minutes

Clapham Common

Clapham Common is located to the south of Battersea, it boast a very large open space which is always used by locals for balls games, cricket, sun bathing and just to enjoy a great open space.

Clapham Common is also known for its Bars, Bars, BARS! With over 30 bars and nightclubs, this area of south London is very popular with the 23-30 year old crowds of young professional. Everything from 80's cheese clubbing and karaoke bars to RnB, Funky House and Old School Garage is on offer. While it's not the biggest clubbing strip in London, Clapham Common offers a more sophisticated crowd and selection of venues. Please remember, you have to be at least 18 years old to legally consume alcohol in the UK. Some establishments enforce a '21 years old and above only' policy and some are for the over 25's only. In either case you will need photo ID with you as almost all venues operate a "No ID no entry" policy and simply looking old enough is usually not enough to get in.

You can also catch the underground from Clapham Common station. This is a Northern Line service that will take you to London Bridge, Bank and Camden Town (among many other locations).

***

VI.4. Avoid poor management

The magic words are: change, emotional needs, motivation, and network support. Presenting your home and supervising your team should look effortless; your management and supervision, start long before the arrival of your guests, and doesn't stop during their stay. When you are singly handling your property, it is a lot harder to manage all aspect that constitute your Hotel Alternative business, from reservation desk, client relations, reviews, social media, property management, marketing to the whole spectrum of exercising great hospitality skills. Nothing is impossible under the sun and managing on your own could be very rewarding, but, only if you really have no choice. Whether you are new to management or not in order to enhance the way you manage your holiday place you should be aware of the emotional needs of the people staying with you. This can be a challenge especially when you have to handle your own emotions, manage your own time, and smile!

Remember that you invited these people to your house, and, most importantly, they are paying guests. From the other hand, when working with other people who are hired to help you, supervision is the key. Sometimes, you can see what the person doing the task can otherwise easily overlook; being house proud yourself can inspire people working with you, as a team, rather than getting on with an odd job that must be done.

Supervising and managing it is all about being aware of the emotional needs of the people you are in charge of, delivering your highest level of commitment yourself. There are many different management approaches and because your Home is open to the world travelers you should take into consideration not only the fact that they are, perhaps, very tired after a long trip, but, also, very different to you. Your job is to make them feel at home. Luckily, there are some fundamental basics that always work. Here it comes:

1. Training yourself and your team to think on your feet and apply appropriate techniques at the right time.
2. Enhancing your people spirit and motivate them on a regular basis, by rewarding them, even for their daily tasks; doesn't need to be much, sometimes a thumbs up or breakfast is enough/ remembering their birthday or going out together for a nice meal after a long week, should show them how much you value their efforts.
3. Motivating people and motivating yourself means that you understand what motivates your people and what motivates you.
4. Leading the way, the right way, all the way, for all your team. There are solutions to apply when keeping the balance in the work space, but the most successful ones are linked to your leadership performances.

I may add that working with your family, it is never going to be easy. Be diplomatic, negotiate your position of authority and do not get upset when your own family will disappoint you. Address the topic quickly; make no compromises as far as your standards are concerned, absolutely never-never, entertain poor management. Be ready to accept a little dent on your ego, this is just a battle you are losing, not the war. All is not lost.

When you feel that rebellious behavior is taking a toll on you, it will become counter-productive and you have to put a stop to it. You can either, hire help outside your family for a while, or take a management course to brush up your skills on managing the young. If neither will work, talk to me, I am a decent listener and I will become your discreet network support. Personally I will relate to your circumstances and together will find the practical steps that will give you the fresh insight to reshaping yourself into the confident relaxed manager you truly are. That always helps.

Learn to use simple techniques to implement both long term and short term motivation, which will guarantee a bond of trust within your team and a positive attitude with your guests. Creating jobs for other people is no longer enough to get the recognition you deserve, in the modern workplace. You should be aware of your people's aspirations, likes and dislikes, but at all times, show them respect. They will return it to you, in many folds!

Have in mind, that you are expected to initiate the positive change for your work environment and that you are bound to deliver the change and manage it, again and again, effortlessly. Remember to Plan your thinking and adapt to every single challenge, gracefully. It took me years to learn this little truth, but it is very liberating.

***

Owners Back Office

VII.1. Availability calendar

An availability calendar is an essential tool which we need to maintain accurate to avoid double bookings. It is nothing more frustrating than not having enough accommodation for your guests. Depending on your marketing strategy and whether you have in mind the bigger picture when you start marketing your property or just go with the flow. If you are buying an advert on one of the major holiday websites, they will offer you a calendar feature which can be up-dated from your own computer, really easy. This will help your advert go up on the search, each time you take a booking and up- date your calendar on their website.

Personally I experience two types of major hazards when accepting bookings from enquiries generated by holiday websites. The first of them is accepting short stays, well in advance. This will limit your availability for longer stays, which will kick in later, closer to arrival, (standard bookings).

People do plan ahead and it is a lot easier for them to book in advance when their stay is shorter (and cheaper). Guests placing their reservation well in advance know the market really well, and, if they need a week end away, they will make the reservation 6 months in advance or more. By accepting a two nights booking, one year in advance, you will limit your option to take a 4 weeks booking closer to the arrival time.

People seeking long term bookings tend to place their reservation closer to their check in time, after they bought their airplane tickets or after everybody in their family, or group, managed to take time off, or when their assignment to a new location was finally confirmed.

While taking into account the advice from the "how to" page of any holiday website, there is no mention of these consumer trends, which may not work to your advantage. Agencies' income is hinges upon the customer's satisfaction and trends, and they will protect their customer's interest to create credibility for themselves. However, while treating their clients with utmost care, property owners are considered simply a six digit reference number, from whom the agency will cash all benefits they can for their advertising.

The property owner will be locked into a contract with very little, if any, protection for their business interest, even they are the apartment supplier, without which the whole process would be impossible.

One of the most hazardous aspects is when you agree to a very relaxed cancellation policy. Everybody will treat you like a hotel, even if you do not have a reception where people could walk in and make last minute reservations, as hotel do. You will be expected to block the dates for bookings that were never paid for and wait (and pray) for the guest to turn up until midnight. There are no guarantees that they will ever arrive and that you will collect the payment.

In case of double bookings, some agencies will make you pay the difference for more expensive accommodation, at one of their listing partners, should you not be able to honor a booking they made outside your knowledge. When they could not find anything else available in their listings, and they forced the booking onto your property calendar, after 2.00PM while you were at the property checking people in. Why? Because they had to convert that enquiry at all cost and make a sale and earn commission.

Most agents run their business from a call centre , they will have a P.O. Box , a virtual, address, while you will have people knocking on your very real front door and little power (if any) to sort out the mess they created for you, into a cross wire communication twist. Guests expecting a whole house for their family and not a tiny hotel room will take their frustrations on you, because you are in front of them, and the agency told them it is your responsibility to find another accommodation for their stay. They will understand what is really happening and they will, eventually, ask for your help and sympathy. How convenient for the agent!

What I learned (please remember this before you sign up with a fancy agency) is that the only thing they really care for, it is not the customer, nor the property owner, but their own commission, and nothing else. May be, you should find a platform when you are in control, and you are treated as a partner by likeminded people who are property owners themselves and they do not take you with a six digit reference number.

***

VII.2.Booking forms

When listing your property with The Hotel Alternative, your back office is constantly improved with practical features like a booking calendar (or availability calendar), booking forms, reports, raports, and other ready to use professional components, or widgets, which are integrated in your property rental page in a matter of a few minutes.

Your back office web based applications are designed to help you market your property from anywhere in the world, and manage your rental business online, with an all- in- one solution that gives you the power to manage enquiries, bookings, payments, and marketing campaigns.

Once payment is made (20% or 50% of the total amount) our booking system will send automatic e-mails to both the guest and the owner. This is the general template:

***

Property Type: Luxury 2 Bed 2 Bath Apartment

Dates: 7 Apr 2012 - 14 Apr 2012

Number of nights: 7 nights

Number of guests: 4 guests

Guest leader name: Samantha Brightman

Booking ID 186884

Booked on the 2 Jan 2012

Payment received: £700.00 from card ending: 465

Balance due: £ 700.00

Total Payment: £1,400.00

Message: Please Remember to contact your guest to arrange a time for the check-in

E-mail: sbrightman@xxxx.com

Phone: 0011387xxxx594

Location of property:

Address: xx, xx, xx,London, United Kingdom

Property type: Entire Apartment

Additional Fees: N/A

Refundable deposit: £300 (credit card authorization only)

Cancellation Policy: Strict

Only Bookings cancelled by the guest up to 2 months before the start of the stay will receive a 50% refund (50% of this amount will be transferred to you)

Cancellations must be made by 12 midday CET (Central European Time) on the appropriate day.

These are your contact details sent to the guest

Phone: +44 (0) 20xxxxxxx7

Email: res@thehotelalaternative.co.uk

If you require assistance with this booking, please contact our Customer Service team via res@thehotelalternative.co.uk or +44 20 33 84 9060

***

VII.3. Turning Enquiries into Bookings

Live, instant bookings, are placed online by guests as a No 1 method when they make reservations for their stay, same way the book their flight. In the unlikely event that you will opt for 'enquiries based model' and not take the benefit of our booking system, there are aspects to ponder over and learn how to turn enquiries into bookings. Sticking yourself like a stamp on your computer screen for hours on end, and answer all enquiries immediately, will definitely help.

I remember those years back, when I was literally like an extension of my desk. My son Michael would finish work and go out for few hours. Coming back he would find me where he left me, at my desk, typing, writing, reading, and working with no breaks. Both, Michael and his younger brother Darie, who was still a student, started looking for solutions to ease the process of bookings and free up my time. They used to say: "Must be a better way of doing this"

Thinking about it, I am not sure how I managed to get bookings, 4 out of 10 enquiries, as a standard, even during quiet seasons, manually, with no system or automated reports! Needless to say, I had no weekends, no holidays, no days out, absolutely nothing but hard work, for very long years. Not sure if my sons' determination to implement a system that works was born out of fear that I will never separate myself from my desk and enjoy little life again. They did everything with such great love that I cannot but top up my maternal love with deep respect and amazement for their hard work, and love them back in many, many folds.

As our audience is the World Wide Web, most common enquiries would come from our Internet marketing campaigns. Also, there will be telephone enquiries from Local Corporation which are looking to accommodate their staff or clients locally, for training courses or events. All inquiries must be answered within 3-5 minutes, the most, while the person placing their enquiry is still online.

To win new business, you should find a way to accommodate all enquiries and even if you do not have enough availability and room for large groups, keep a positive attitude and go outside your comfort zone by placing their enquiries with other landlords or members of the Hotel Alternative community.

All enquiries should be answered professionally, using a template format that includes: requested dates, number of guests, rates, full payment conditions and full rental conditions (very clearly stated in all communication and on the website)

Of course, it is a lot easier and far more efficient to insert all details in your live calendar so your guests could place the booking online, at their own leisure.

When you received their deposit, the guest received an email to confirm their booking, simultaneously. From this point on, a relation will start building up, from small questions, to big, generous answers, mainly via e-mail, but expect phone calls from people who never booked a private house before. There will be further automated communication from our booking system to confirm details such as:

standard arrival time

number of guests and extra beds

confirmation of received payment

booking arrival and departure dates

amount and means by which the balance should be paid

when and if damage deposit is expected

details of how to reach the property

contact details of the Greeter meeting the guest at the property

terms and condition of business

A few days before arrival is due, our system will sent a friendly reminder with directions to the property, address, and a reminder to call us one hour before their agreed check in time and so on. Nothing is left at chance, and if the guest needs transfer from the airport, we are happy to arrange a taxi to wait for them by the arrivals' gate with their name clearly written on a board to make sure, guests will be looked after and care for, in the same way you would care for your own family.

Sometimes, guests may write with additional questions which will give you the chance to build a report with your guests, get to know them and let them to know you and your home, which will help them imagine the whole experience from the moment they will pass the threshold of your home, which, by now, they absolutely acknowledge, it is NOT a hotel room, but the whole house!

VII.4. Accepting Reservations

Accepting Reservations is all about being ready to welcome new visitors to your house and accepting bookings live, online. Once you accept a new reservation, remember all the right reasons people choose your place and why their choice will make you proud of your home. In return, the way you care for your guests will give them all reasons they need to come back, or not.

I have a standard short list of practical tasks and should be crystal clear to all property owners running The Hotel Alternative that this is a routine exercise, for each time you accepted another booking:

1. Meet and greet the guests upon arrival and give them the keys together with your best –friendly- welcome-smile!

2. Be available and reliable in case of an emergency during their stay.

3. Collect reviews at the end of the stay

4. Check property and contents for damage

5. Clean the apartment thoroughly, change the bed linen and towels and get the property ready in good time for the next guest.

Also, you should make your conditions of business very clear from the very beginning, and, insist that your guests read your terms and conditions, or house rules, before placing their booking. This is your obligation as a host. What follows is just a sample for your inspiration.

Sample: **Terms and Conditions**

Conditions

You agree to use the property as a single hotel dwelling or short term accommodation and for no other purpose, including but not limited to: business purposes, subletting, keeping of live animals, proof address or to pursue any sort of application for you or others using the property address, unless written consent has been given by us beforehand.

You agree to do your utmost to look after the property and contents so it may be returned to us in the same condition as found. You acknowledge that if any fault/damage is caused or found it is your responsibility to report it to us as soon as possible and that failure to do so can place you liable for all costs. In cases of severe damage to the apartment and/or contents where such action were intentional or of a completely careless nature, all liability for all costs will be taken by you, including but not limited to: cost of repairs/replacement of items, cost of relocation for future guests (where applicable), cost of labor (where applicable) and all admin costs arising from such cases. We reserve the right to determine what a suitable replacement of a damaged item is.

You acknowledge that the number of guests in your party will not exceed that stated on your reservation and that no extra persons will stay at the property during your period of rental, unless first agreed so by us and any extra cost necessary have been settled by you. With the exception of day visitors that must adhere to the following rules; (a) All visitors must depart from the property by 10.30pm (22:30 hr) and cannot return until 8:30 am (08:30hr) the following day;

You agree to respect the privacy of other guests and not cause any disturbances (within reasons) that may otherwise affect their stay. Especially you fully agree that no loud music will be played after 10.00 PM (22.00hr) and no parties will be held on the premises. You understand and agree that smoking inside the premises is against the law and that by doing so you will be in breach of the said law and take you will take full liability for it.

Payment Conditions

- 50% upfront payment required to secure reservation. Balances settled on arrival.
- Any applicable fees must also be settled at the time of booking.
- Payments cannot be taken unless availability for your rental is first confirmed.

Cancellation Conditions

- In case of cancellations, modifications or no-show, 50% of the reservation is non refundable.
- Any applicable fees are non refundable.

VII.5. Cancellation policy

There is much flexibility when deciding on your cancellation policy and I will mention a few to choose from. Please have in mind that you are not a hotel where people just walk in. Your bookings are made well in advance, from one year to 6 weeks and your occupancy level it is not supported by 'last minute' bookings.

In general, best Cancellation Policy for The Hotel Alternative is based on commitment and fairness:

- In case of cancellations, modifications or no-show, 20% of the reservation is non refundable.
- Any applicable fees are non refundable.

Feel free to use any other types of cancellation policies that suit your guests and property, and make sure you choose your Cancellation Policy before your advert goes live.

1. Relaxed:

- If a guest cancels their booking up to 2 weeks before the start of their stay, they will receive 100-85% refund
- If a guest cancels their booking up to 1 week before the start of their stay, they will receive a 50% refund

Cancellations must be made by 12.00 pm, GMT

2. Medium:

- If a guest cancels their booking up to 1 month before the start of their stay, they will receive a 85% refund

Cancellations must be made by 12 noon GMT

3. Strong:

- If a guest cancels their booking up to 2 months before the start of their stay, they will receive a 50% refund. Cancellations must be made by 12.00 pm, GMT

4. Strict:

- If a guest cancels their booking up to 2 months before the start of their stay, they will receive no refund but an alternative date when the booking can be reinstated subject to availability. Cancellations must be made by 12.00 pm, GMT

5. Non-Refundable for all Advance bookings

***

The Hotel Alternative: Daily

VIII.1. Work smart and dress for success

Thinking ahead is the middle name of The Hotel Alternative. Ask yourself this:

What are your guests' expectations?

No matter what they want from their own home in real life, or how much they paid or where is their temporary accommodation located, your guests want to move into a pristine environment.

They will expect to find absolutely no traces of other people living at the property before them. They do not want to see different type of hangers left behind by the previous guests from clothes they bought in London, nor do they want to smell previous guests last dinner. Cleaning should be professionally done each time somebody checks out and if you hire someone to clean for you, you should be vetting and supervising their work very seriously. The property will not be ready for occupancy unless you are satisfied with the end result.

What are guests' expectations from you?

Make sure that you get the property ready for their arrival and dress smart yourself. This is my personal view: You are a business person, and it is your duty to introduce yourself and your home to your guests at your best behavior and image. While your house is immaculate, you should be confident and pleasant because you are the human face of your business rental. Preparing yourself should be similar to going to a meeting with your next employer, so, dress for success. Do not dismiss the importance of your own image because your house value will only go up and the feedback from your guests will match exactly that.

***

VIII.2. Check in to check out: one journey

Meet and Greet is the most effective way to introduce your house to your guests. Finding few minutes to welcome them it will make the difference for the rest of their stay and the whole experience more valuable. Treating your guests like you know them and you are happy to see them, it will pay off in the long run. There are particular details to be explained, where everything can be found, showing them round the house, room by room, how to use appliances, how to switch on and off electrical goods, where to find everything they need during their stay, like extra blankets or towels, etc.

When you hand over the key, you should try to be relaxed and happy, because now you are setting the mood for your relation with your guests.

Even if they are very tired, after a long trip, you will have this chance to make a good impression, show them how important is their wellbeing for you and how much you want them to have a good time during their stay. This initial contact could save you unwanted late-night or early-morning calls from the guests when they get frustrated for not finding soap or towels. 'Meet and Greet' and you will get to know them and trust them with your house keys.

Of course, there are other methods of giving access to your property but I will not consider them unless it is absolutely a one off situation when you are held in traffic or on a holiday yourself. As a standard, we explained already at the time of booking, to our guests, that we do not have a reception or concierge on standby, but we are happy to wait for them and not the other way around; should they be able to call us one hour before their agreed check in time, as this will give us enough time to arrive at the property ourselves.

Do this first bit right, and you will establish a solid relationship with your guests, agree on a check out time that suits them, sign the paperwork (not more than one page, please) check their ID, collect the balance on their total payment, and give them the chance to relax themselves. You will probably not need to carry out the check out procedure, because, your relation is based on trust and both guests and home owners want to build a good relationship and stay friends.

Meet and Greet is a crucial moment because they will tell other people how well you welcomed them, after a long trip, how 'at home' you help them feel, against their anxiety of not knowing where they are going to sleep, if the picture on your add were accurate, and so on. Giving your guests the chance to celebrate their choice for your property instead of a hotel room, it is emotionally charged and liberating.

Imagine that all the way from their country until this moment, and, perhaps, the thought of the 'one off chance' that things will go wrong, your property could be the wrong choice and ruin their trip, was in the back of their mind. They are here now, they are really' wowed' by the property, your personality and they feel safe. They will, definitely, share their first impression with their friends, in person, or on the internet. They will go on Twitter and facebook, with cool photos and links and if you are doing this right, your property will become a very appealing commodity, worldwide.

On the surfaces 'Meet and greet' appears to be the moment when you hand over the key but, actually, there is a lot more to it because first impression counts and a simple smile could bring extraordinary positive energy between people; it is a key moment when your guests are connecting emotionally with both home and home owner.

Welcoming, shaking hands and making friends is of the essence for any hospitality exercise and if you are not happy meeting new people, you have to learn how to connect. Your care and consideration for your guests is the core of the hotel alternative model and you have this one chance to open your door and smile to new opportunities.

***

Sample: Check In Guidance

We hope you are as excited about your trip to London as we are to welcome you.

We would kindly like to remind you of some important steps you should take in advance of your arrival at our apartments to ensure we can provide you with the best service possible.

This short guide includes:

Check-in instruction

How to arrange airport pickup

Directions when using public transport

Directions when arriving by car from abroad

Useful things you should remember to pack

Important:

Keys are collected directly from the property.

Once you have arrived in London, please call us when you are 1 hour away.

Call once again when you are outside the property and one of our property managers will come and meet you. Our telephone number: +44 (0) 203 384 9060

Our standard check-in is from 2.00pm until 6.00pm but we are happy to accommodate your arrival outside these hours so long as you inform us in advance. This is to minimize your awaiting time before you can check in.

Please remember to bring both your confirmation and receipt with you as you will need it to check in.

Step 1

It is very important that you provide us with a contact telephone number for a mobile/cellular telephone that you will have with you while in the UK. It is also very helpful to give us an expected arrival time.

Step 2

Once you have reached London please call us when you are 1 hour away. Our office number is +44 (0) or +44 (0)

If you are arriving after 18.00 our office may be closed in which case you will need to call +44 (0), this is 24 hour emergency number that you can use throughout your stay so please make a note of it.

Step 3

Once you are in front of the property call once again on the above number and we will send someone downstairs to let you in.

Airport Pickup

We are happy to arrange airport pick up for you, provided by a local taxi company. We do not charge a fee for this service and you will have to pay all costs to the driver directly. To use this service you need to provide us with complete flight details, number of passengers and number of suitcases and contact number. We will then make all necessary arrangements for you. The driver will wait for you outside the terminal at the taxi pick up point.

Directions

From Heathrow airport

Make your way to the underground station (metro) in terminal 3. From here take the Piccadilly Line (dark blue) towards Cockfosters. Disembark at Hammersmith Station and take the district line (green) towards Upminster. Disembark at Victoria Station and make your way out of the underground station and into the railway station above by following the signs for national rail. From Victoria train station take the train for 1 stop to Battersea Park

From Gatwick Airport

From Gatwick airport you can make you way to our apartments in the following ways.

Gatwick Express trains take you directly to Victoria Station. From Victoria train station take the train for 1 stop to Battersea Park Station.

From Stanstead Airport

Upon leaving Stanstead airport, please make your way to Stanstead airport Rail Station by following the signs for 'National Rail'. Please take the National Express East Anglia service towards Liverpool Street and disembark at Tottenham Hale Station. From here take the underground (metro) on the Victoria Line (light blue) towards Brixton and disembark at Victoria Station. Make your way out of the underground station and into the railway station above by following the signs for national rail. From Victoria Train Station take the train for 1 stop to Battersea Park Station.

From Luton Airport

From Luton Airport take the Route Express Bus 888 service to Luton Airport Parkway Rail Station. Take the First Capital Connect service towards Brighton and disembark at St Pancreas International. From here please walk to Kings Cross St Pancreas (these two station are linked, you simply need to follow the signs for Kings Cross St Pancreas). From Kings Cross St Pancreas take the underground (metro) on the Victoria Line (light blue) towards Brixton and disembark at Victoria Station. Make your way out of the underground station and into the railway station above by following the signs for national rail. From Victoria Train Station take the train for 1 stop to Battersea Park Station.

From City Airport

From London City airport make your way to the DLR station. Take the DLR service towards Bank DLR Station and Disembark at Canning Town Underground Station. Take the underground (metro) on the Jubilee Line (grey) towards Wembley Park or Stanmore or Willesden Green and disembark at London Bridge. From London Bridge Underground make your way to the train station above by following the 'National Rail' signs. From London

Bridge Rail Station take the train towards Victoria Station and disembark at Battersea Park Station.

From St Pancreas International / Kings Cross

From St Pancreas International please walk to Kings Cross St Pancreas (these two station are linked, you simply need to follow the signs for Kings Cross St Pancreas). From Kings Cross St Pancreas take the underground (metro) on the Victoria Line (light blue) towards Brixton and disembark at Victoria Station. Make your way out of the underground station and into the railway station above by following the signs for national rail. From Victoria Train Station take the train for 1 stop to Battersea Park Station.

From Dover

Take the M20 towards London. Stay on the M20 until you reach A20. Take the A20 all the way into New Cross (London). From New Cross take the A202 all the way to xxx

By Taxi

Our address is: XXXX

The following map may also be useful:

http://www.thehotelalternative.co.uk/

From Victoria Station

From Victoria Train Station take the train for 1 stop to Battersea Park Station.

You should also know that you only need to travel to Zones 1 & 2. For an easy way to plan all your journeys in London we recommend you use http://journeyplanner.tfl.gov.uk

Things you should remember:

We recommend that you remember to bring your own power adaptors for UK sockets. We may be able to provide you with some; however stock is always limited and you should not assume we can provide them.

Please remember that you will need a valid credit/debit card with you to check in (card holder has to be present). A copy will be kept for the entirety of your stay as a guarantee against possible damage to contents. However, we reserve the right to request at out discretion a cash deposit of 30 GBP per person to be kept until checkout.

Each apartment comes with linen and towels for each guest so you do not have to bring your own. We also provide tea, coffee and sugar as standard in each apartment. High speed broadband internet access (Wi-Fi) is available in each apartment and is included in the price.

Should you need any further help or perhaps you have further questions please do not hesitate to contact us. You can do so by calling +44 (0) or by emailing us at res@thehotelalternative.co.uk

***

VIII.3. Collecting payments: deposits versus trust

Booking is only confirmed when payment is made. All payments must be upfront, without exceptions and this is a cardinal rule. There are no exceptions. You do not take a booking without payment, ever. When you commit yourself and accept a new booking, you block the dates so nobody else can secure the same dates. At the same time, it is just fair that a commitment is made at the other end, and you receive a minimum deposit of 20% or 50%.

Second part of this cardinal rule is to collect the balance for the whole amount, on or before your guests check in. Make NO exceptions when payments are involved. Do not check in anyone, without full payment in clear funds for the whole amount. While 20% - 50% of the total amount was already collected at the time of booking, the balance should be collected at check in time, at the latest. On very rare occasions, if arrival is after midnight and there are small kids, depending on your own judgment, try to arrange payment before their arrival; or you could return next morning, before they go out, and complete the payment. Delaying any longer, it will create an embarrassing situation when you are chasing them for payment and interfering with their plans. So be polite but firm and collect the balance when it is due, at check in, and do not hand over your keys unless payment is settled as agreed. If you are taking a damage deposit, which should be refunded when they leave your property, please make sure you explain that you expect the house to be as clean as found and give out a receipt to say exactly that:

***

"Damage deposit of £400.00

From Mr and Mrs ____________________ of ____________________________

Subject to the property being left as clean as found; all eventual breakages or damages will be deducted.

Signature of guests____

Signature of Property owner____

Date ____"

***

Because having people staying at your property is not just about making a profit but mostly helping your guests to feel at home and choose to come back, you should always try to take damage deposit money out of the equation and replace it with trust.

Each case should be treated with upmost fairness and each case should be judged on their merits. You can suggest that small eventual breakages could be replaced by the existing guests, for the benefit of the next guests who, in all fairness, should enjoy same level of comfort, instead of charging them or deducting the said damages from their deposit.

If you supply a telephone line or a computer, you can limit the level of usage or arrange a pay-as- you- go option, instead of disputing the value at later stage. I would judge each case individually but ease the process with kindness.

Over one year, from one property you could take an average of 75 bookings. If each damage deposit is about £300.00, this means that you could have a client account where you keep these deposits of about £2,000 per month. Your bank will like the spirit of it, but your guests will feel, perhaps, very anxious during their stay and not worthy of your trust. However, if you do not want to take a damage deposit but still protect your position, take details of a valid credit card and keep them on file, same way as a hotel would do, it is a lot easier for everyone especially for your guests who could be nervous that they will never recover their refundable deposit.

Personally, I do not want to collect any additional payments but details of a valid credit card, because it is less paperwork involved and mainly because I do not want to dent my guests' ego. A 'deposit free attitude', will boost your genuine welcome, and generate positive vibes because there is trust. Chances are that damages will not occur, because these people have a house themselves and they try to put themselves in your shoes.

When you take a damage deposit, you will slightly distance your guests by not trusting them; as a secondary effect, will make them think they are not really welcome in your house. If you like the guests, you should ask yourself: "These are my new friends, how can I ask them to pay for my trust?" In all honesty, while you judge each situation on its own merits, you should not do something you will not like other people to do to yourself if the situation was reversed.

***

VIII.4. Skills and confidence

We're in a profession that offers others a travel product which is unique because of the skill and knowledge home owners bring to the table. So we really should understand the benefits of being trusted by someone who is an expert traveler but is relying on a wonderful concept which is ultimately created by skilled people for smart people.

Practice makes perfect, as they say, but please allow yourself time to feel comfortable within your new found identity: a person of many talents.

Your main talent lies in providing a home away from home for total strangers, who will choose to trust you unconditionally in three different areas of your hospitality business

1. trust you with their money, as they made a payment to an individual they never met before

2. trust your entrepreneurial skills because you created their home for them entirely, from finding the property, developing into a real home, choosing the right feature, the right furniture, the adequate kitchen and color scheme

3. trust your managerial skills because you are the manager of your own boutique hotel alternative; during their stay at your property they will be depending on your skills from sourcing the right suppliers, polite staff ,comfortable beds to paying your bills in time, just to mention a few of the ingredients that make you a good manager.

To reach that point when you are a hospitality expert, it will take more than passing an exam each quarter or academic year. You will pass an exam each time a new group of people will be reaching for the threshold of your property and you will open the door for them. How many examinations (actually, I should mention thorough examination) in a year? We are talking of an average of 72 exams which you pass with flying colors each year, for each property that you have live on the hospitality map.

As intimidating as this may look to most people, there is no better credentials for your profession than the durable relation you create with your visitors, the synergy that comes within, when total strangers become your friends and they recognize your skills and respect you as a person of many talents. You may think by now that it is a great privilege to offer a home away from home to people you never dreamed of meeting and knowing and that your property is a winner because of its location, uniqueness, charming character or local area. Surprisingly, your best asset is not your home, or your data base of thousand of clients, or your lifestyle, but your own Confidence.

Your personal notes:

How to conquer Everest

IX.1. Reviews

We are a fast growing group of property providers offering online reservations for our luxury apartments, houses, condos, cottages and exclusive villas, from as little as two nights to several months stays. We are serving private clients, corporations and travel agencies from Europe, US and emerging markets. The only way people from different continents could place their reservations for our properties are online bookings.

There are thousands and thousands of hotel chains, international brands, and each time somebody will place a booking online, they will make their decisions based on their own experience or other people's experience, posted online. Generically they are called Reviews and they are very instrumental in placing reservations online. When published on Trip Advisor, reviews can make or break your reputation as a provider within the Hospitality industry.

There are lots of other similar websites acting as a' Review Centre' but Trip Advisor is the largest community of real people, just like you and me, with over 20 million members, sharing their experiences online. Publishing their posts, travelers provide unbiased assistance for other accommodation seekers to discover what is right for them. Our level of bookings is thriving since we signed up with Trip Advisor.

But do not take my word for it; see what our guests had to say:

★★★★★

"*We stayed at the apartment on business and Darie and the team were very helpful with all our needs and requests. The apartment is spacious, clean with modern decor - the perfect base. There's lots of facilities' nearby including pubs, restaurants and a supermarket, so everything you need is close to hand. Definitely recommended!!*"

★★★★★

"The apartment is beautifully done and was a great base for our weekend in London. There isn't a tube station close by but you can get buses from outside. It rained all weekend so we just used taxi's everywhere! The owners were very kind and let us have a late check out too which was great as our train wasn't until 2pm on Sunday. I'd highly recommend staying here."

★★★★

"Hi, I stayed in this apartment with my friends and it was a great place to stay, very clean and the garden space was a great extra, very easy booking and made to feel very welcome in a great part of London, hope to be back very soon."

"Hello, We were in the apartment with two bathrooms and three bedrooms. We were five, and with the cleanliness of the equipment and the grass sunbathing very satisfied. A contact person was very quick and easy to spot. The connection to the City was on the bus (bus stop very close) very well. The single glazing of the windows was of course the noise of the street by well, that was a bedroom for a little noisy. Otherwise we were very pleased with everything and would book the apartment again."

"We just had a fabulous stay at Battersea Park. The Pictures shown of the apartment are true and we were really impressed by the 5 star appearance.

We travelled with a group of young children who could not believe their eyes. Michael and Darie were very helpful and they went the extra mile to make us feel like home. The bus stop is only a minute walk away and to get to the heart of London it only takes 10 min. The Kids had a great time in London and so did we ;)"

***

IX.2. Customers' feedback and referrals

While reviews are unbiased evaluations for your product and service, and are in effect, recommendations that help you attract, engage and retain more customers; referrals are the thumbs up, the mother of any reviews. They have been round before the internet era, and they will be above any other marketing tools in existence, at all times. When counting my blessings I am thinking of all the people who recommended my house to their friends and family. I do not find enough words for how grateful I am.

Both my sons are trying to convince me to spend more on SEO. I would love to, but quotations are very volatile; it is impossible to decide on a marketing budget as starts 'from' £10,000 but nobody wants to commit in writing to measurable results. The truth may be brutal but any advert I ever placed in local or professional magazines and other traditional publishing materials, never brought any new clients. The adverts I paid for were really to help the editors and their publications and I did not expect any results.

However, if I distribute £10,000 a year by rewarding loyal clients in any way I can, reducing their rates, giving them a free day at the end of their stay or simply contributing to their favorite charity, it is a far more fulfilling method of utilizing my marketing budget.

Customers' Feedback tips:

1. Regardless of the size of your operation, visitor's feedback is very important to your growth and profitability. Improving customer satisfaction and generating repeat business are door openings to your great reputation. A good reputation means repeat business, less marketing, increase of sales. And so we understand each other, repeat business doesn't just happen. You have to work constantly hard at it.

2. However difficult may be to read your reviews, calm down and just imagine, it is

Not personal to you. After you read the whole text, make it into smaller paragraphs and dismantle the message into small positive messages.

3. When asking for your guests' opinion you show them how important they are

to you, because they truly are . When listening to them you are not only understanding their needs but their expectations as well, which is a win-win situation.

They win your attention but you win their business and prove that you truly value them.

4. There are two Types of feedback: Honest and Malicious.

Honest feedback is what you need to listen to, very carefully and say thank you

for it. Because you have the ability to learn fast, adapt your business to your

Customers' needs, you become more profitable. Simple facts which cost you

next to nothing, when addressed to your client's satisfaction, will make a whole world of difference.

There are three categories of Honest Feedback: positive, neutral, or negative.

Positive feedback constitutes all the likes, but has nothing to contribute to your business except for the 'feel good factor' that you are very good at what you do. Well done! Positive feedback, should be used as testimonials, which are very powerful credentials to be market it to new customers

Example ***

"We loved our stay in this apartment. It was very spacious, clean and very close to the bus stop. We already recommended it on facebook to our friends."

***

Negative feedback is a good tool to better your service, free consultancy actually, pointing out all the dislikes, what you should improve and maybe how to do it.

***

Example

"We were in the apartment with two bathrooms and three bedrooms. We were five, and with the cleanliness of the equipment and the grass sunbathing very satisfied. A contact person was very quick and easy to spot. The connection to the City was on the bus (bus stop very close) very well. The single glazing of the windows was of course the noise of the street by well, that was a bedroom for a little noisy. Otherwise we were very pleased with everything and would book the apartment again."

<u>*Our answer and actions:*</u>

"Thank you for leaving us with feedback on your stay. We are delighted to hear you had a great time staying with us. We are also aware that sometimes it can be a little noisy and we will be adding another level of glazing to all windows to ensure a quiet and peaceful stay from now on. We hope to see you again soon."

It was not easy, but Michael found an ingenious way to install further secondary glazing with a company specialized in Grade II Listed properties.

Neutral feedback is sent out to you when people were not impressed but they want to reply to your request anyway; usually means they will come back. You will have enough time to think why they weren't impressed and how to improve your service; put even the insignificant wrong, right, and as a result, you will do better by your clients.

***

Example

"Everything went well, very responsive and well organized. We were 6 adults with 3 kids. The only thing, reading lamps in the small bedroom are missing and coat storage in the ceiling would be helpful."

<u>*Our answer and actions:*</u>

"Hi,

Thank you for your feedback, we have now replaced our wall mounted lamps with reading lamps in all bedrooms and a coat hanger by the main entrance. We are happy to hear that you are satisfied with our service and we hope to see you again soon.

Kind Regards, Darie"

***

Reviews could be signed or anonymous, they all mean well as long as you can see the constructive message. Read them with your mind and not with your heart. It is not personal, do not be offended by other people's opinion (easier said than done, I know that); after all, they all took the trouble to write to you. Smile. You are on...the Internet!

Malicious reviews do exist and could come from unfair competition. Doesn't happen that often, but be aware. It is mostly signed with fake names.

You have nothing to be afraid, request feedback from every single guests!

Make a good habit and always request your visitor's feedback.

The feedback process can be easily initiated by e-mail, phone, or in person.

You could set up a standard e-mail request on the departure day, or simply ask your guests how were they while staying at your house and when are you going to see them again. You can use this moment to take their next reservation and block off their dates, just provisionally.

Feedback can take many forms, depending on the location and size of your Home. Methods of collecting feedback could include comment cards left inside the property for the guests to fill them out during their stay and to be collected at check out time. You could treat your feedback as an online survey, when you sent out an electronic feedback form. When setting up your online feedback form, bear in mind that some people may feel more comfortable to sign anonymously, so you should create this option.

Best of, if you have the chance to speak to your customers without intruding their privacy – ask them few short questions in person or over the phone. Once you have initiated the feedback process, make it easy for customers to choose their favorite method, in a way that is preferable to them (online, post, by hand, or by phone).

When people aren't giving you feedback, because they are too busy, you may need to offer an incentive, to qualify for the loyalty voucher or allow them to enter into a prize draw. Never underestimate the importance of feedback request. If you fail to place the feedback request your guests will just assume that you're not interested in their opinion and as a result, they will lose interest in you. It is a two way street and courtesies are always paying off handsomely.

Furthermore, your request gives you the opportunity to find out, for free, what otherwise large companies are paying substantial sums of money to mirror their products and services. Your paying guests will tell you, FOR FREE, what else they would like to spend their money on or what changes will make them spend even more, while staying with you next time. Usually, such changes will make your service more appealing and enter a gold category: “value for money” - when you are “value for money” in your visitors' books, you are guaranteed a next time visit from them or their friends or family. Beside, those changes will be easy to implement. Worth every penny!

Perhaps you are wondering what area can be improved and where are your services lacking. To create new ideas for your product and additional services, you can initiate a customer survey. Carry out market research, in-house, is a more evolved tool that could also help you understand your market. When even a small proportion of clients wanted the same product or service, let's say, they suggested you to provide for them the morning newspaper, this might highlight an unfulfilled need. Could your current offerings be diversified to meet their need and reach new level of satisfaction? Of course they could. Buy the newspaper, put it under their door and you will be making the news!

***

Example

"Dear Alicja,

Thank you for your stay at the Shakespeare Villa (Garden) vacation rental from Sun, 05 Aug 2012 to Sun, 12 Aug 2012. We hope you had a great stay.

You have earned 70.00 GBP towards your next stay as part of our Loyalty Program!

Next time you book a place, remember to quote RTON01 for the discount to be validated.

The Hotel Alternative Loyalty Program

Earn 5% (or up to a maximum of £200) on each reservation to be used on your next stay. Simply quote your Voucher Code when placing your next booking with us. T&C apply: Selected properties only. Voucher is non-transferable. One time use, balance cannot be carried onto next voucher. Voucher Code: MARTON01

Voucher Value: 70.00 GBP

We would appreciate any comments that you might have. Please take a moment to share your experience with other travelers on TripAdvisor and Flipkey.

http://www.flipkey.com/o/411427/

If you need a place in the future, you can make availability requests at our website at http://www.thehotelalternative.co.uk

Thanks for being a loyal customer. We hope you enjoy this discount on a growing selection of properties displaying the Loyalty Programme* logo.

Why not visit our international property portal?

www.thehotelalternative.co.uk by Luxury Residential

Kind Regards from London,

Front Desk Team

THE HOTEL ALTERNATIVE

***

Please e-mail me

To find out about our Loyalty Program

Or

to redeem your Voucher

Marina@AwayFromHome-book.com

IX.3. The Hotel Alternative Loyalty Program

I learned a lot from both my sons, as they are very kind and they would go hungry to give to others less fortunate or in need. Once we had a large family (with 7 children) staying at our house, for Christmas, and they did not realized that shops will be closed that day, even though we told them that business hours will be limited. They rang me to ask something in their Latin language and I gathered that they wanted to know where they can have a meal because everything was shut.

We brought most of our food to their apartment and when they returned, hungry and frustrated and with no hope for a meal anytime soon, they found the dinner table dressed for celebration and the food in the oven. They were on the phone again, but this time very happy and even though we could not understand their language and definitely they did not understand ours, their happy meal was one of the biggest rewards I ever had.

Perhaps words are not enough to say thank you to our clients anyway, and small gesture could go a long way, regardless they referred further business or come back and stay with us again and again. What is to be encouraged, at all times and by all means, is our clients' loyalty.

Outsourcing our clients loyalty will help diversify our client base and increase our standards of offerings. There are three distinctive methods to attract more business, and all are nothing but a balancing act between our products and our clients' budgetary requirements:

1. Incentive Sales

2. Loyalty Program

3. Reward Program

Any incentives can be seamlessly integrated to deliver attractive rates to a value-conscious clientele, in a digital era where buying online products is the new culture and have a very competitive edge. Regardless of which of the three methods you apply for your property, you will acquire more customers and treated well, they will generate repeat business.

To retain customers, we motivate profitable customer behavior, which will guarantee a consistent share of our market and drive up sales and profits. We started a simple competition where exiting clients enter automatically to win a week free accommodation, for six people, at one of our properties in London. On the 30th October, we have a night out with residing guests and they draw the winner. It is fun and over an exciting dinner, we make more friends.

The winner could give the proceeds to a charity of their choice, if they are not going to be in London again soon. Loyalty works both ways and it is not only about getting more, but mainly about being able to give back more.

All loyalty solutions are very effective and The Hotel Alternative started a new Loyalty program this summer which gives 5% back, either to the returning customer or a charity of their choice. We do value our clients' loyalty and they can see in our attitude that the extra miles to go, are really to meet their precise needs and to measure our customer care and fulfillment with an accurate scale.

Offering our genuine consideration and emotional involvement there is a minimal impact on valuable internal resources and Loyalty, should always be a two way street.

"To say thank you to our guests we have introduced the Loyalty Voucher, a simple and yet rewarding program that offers you 5%* of the value of your original reservation to be used against your next stay with us. For example, if you place a booking worth £400, you will receive a voucher worth £20 for your next stay. Use it on your next booking when selecting any property displaying the 'Loyalty Voucher' logo.

*The value of the voucher cannot exceed 5% or 200.00 GBP (whichever comes first)

Terms &Conditions

1. The voucher is non-transferable and can only be used by you. You are welcome to use the voucher when placing a reservation for a friend or family i.e a gift which is settled by you. 2. Value of voucher is calculated from the rental rates and excludes fees or taxes 3.Only one voucher per reservation, vouchers cannot be combined to increase the discount value of a reservation, nor can they be used more than once. 4. Participating properties only. 5. Voucher cannot be exchanged for refunds or cash-back. 6. The Hotel Alternative reserves the right to retract the offer or void vouchers at our discretion. 7. The Hotel Alternative reserves the right to cancel or amend the terms and conditions and participation of the 'Loyalty Voucher' at any time without notice.

***

IX.4. Knowing for knowing

If you are a landlord and ask me how to do what you love when you have no support from your bank, or anyone else for that matter, you have got my undivided attention. It is an upside down economic climate and most people start feeling powerless, as if they lost a main body function. When Beethoven lost his hearing he didn't lose his music. He accomplished his artistic maturity.

Likewise, your passion for property will stay with you and reach maturity when joining our growing community of home owners passionately running The Hotel Alternative. I want to share with you everything I learned in the last two decades from different countries, and I would like to learn from you, regardless where you are coming from. When sharing your knowledge it is not important where you are coming from but what you have learned from it, and where you are going with what you have learned.

Let me ask you this: Where are you going? Do you have a plan? Talk to me now while I am taking notes, because next thing I will do is look for a solution for you. I learned this: there are no problems in real world, only solutions to different circumstances, and circumstances are changing constantly. Personally I am unfazed by unpredictability and immune to instability, as they are essential components of life's dynamic.

What do you want from your property? The principle of The Hotel Alternative is based on sharing and it is called 'Knowing for Knowing'. Our booking system will make your property available for reservations with an estimated half a million relocation and travel agents, distributing your property to accommodation seekers worldwide. Our support team is just one click or call away from you, 365 days a year.

A smart phone or tablet is all you need to get connected with me. Mobile is the magic word for our digital era. I am like you, always on the go, and like our guests, always travelling. You have instant access to your property's description, images, rates, and availability across all your channels, while maintaining full control over your content at anytime.

My business model offers a simple but powerful way to manage your property distribution online, and I am giving you the key to turn your life round. Our online back office is very friendly and offers you complete control over your availability. You can simply focus on managing your property or developing your portfolio while I bring the bookings in.

For all property owners, it is FREE to join. Why? Right now, we are looking to increase our network because we do not have enough properties to cover demand from existing bookings, from referrals, from tweets', blogs and quality accommodation seekers!
Can this get any better? Yes, because you become part of an exclusive community of entrepreneurs, property experts, media moguls and thousands of landlords who share the knowledge. No big, loud seminars, sitting on chairs for hours, we just get together once in a while, taking turns in hosting our gatherings, on 'knowing for knowing' basis.
We will stay by you, as close or as far as you want us to be.

What to expect? When you decide to venture into the hospitality market waters, don't expect me to tell you what you want to hear, but the truth. You already know how hard life can be when you are on your own, alienated and without the network support that is right for you. I am a very good listener, and you will have my undivided attention.

The Hotel Alternative is also keeping you in the loop, inside the very fabric of our industry and connecting you with other smart entrepreneurs like yourself.
I have planted the seeds of The Hotel Alternative in my heart first, and sharing my concept further requires focus and an open mind attitude from all home owners taking part. There is an organic need to grow together and create our own network support.
We are planning carefully our future as The Hotel Alternative Community is expanding at a steady, healthy pace.

Get involved, you can put your personal mark, regardless of how out of reach may sound right now! It is just natural to feel powerless during difficult times. Remember, when Beethoven lost his hearing completely, at the end of the premiere of his Ninth Symphony, he was unable to hear people applauding him frenetically and he realized his success only when he turn around to see the audience. He had tears of joy coming down on his face. Same way, when you will finish your project, you will turn round to see your talents' recognition, and hundreds of people being grateful for what you are creating for them. Get ready to write your first symphony!

Start you Action Plan Now

And e-mail me with any questions

Marina@AwayFromHome-book.com

Run your portfolio as a successful Family Business

X.1. First property

Depending where you want to operate your rental property from, there are new challenges that you can make work to your advantage. If you are in Great Britain, current sterling exchange rates are a phenomenal attraction for foreign visitors. From the other hand, the influx of economic migrants from Eastern European Countries has been paving the road for a healthy 'Value for money' trend within the UK tourism. Keeping the labor cost low and productivity high is the best kept secret for rates to stay competitively low.

In the United Kingdom, there is a track record of promoting liberalization and deregulation where this unleashes competition, stimulates better services and economic growth. Our Queen is not only an inspiration for us, but a visionary. Her Majesty protects entrepreneurial spirit and trust smalls businesses to bring wealth to the local economy. There are tremendous tax advantages to those who dare.

To run a furnished holiday home business is not only challenging but most of all, very satisfactory. There is support from local authorities, free mentoring from experienced entrepreneurs and demand from customers, and, yes, plenty of opportunities, should you decide to invest in the property market, you should definitely invest in Great Britain.

When choosing your property, make sure that you put yourself into your clients' shoes. The property should be located near prestigious landmarks, flag restaurants and have easy access to tourist attractions. Your local area should be the busy and your property should be located within reach of most important places to be found in the whole of the city, or county. When the neighbouring area of your property does not have the same level of prestige as the city area, it is very important to choose a good area in terms of entertainment! A leafy district in a big metropolis will always be bursting with exciting events, shopping malls and attractions. As long as your property is part of a district with good transport links to the city centre, your guests will love it.

In each country there are places of interest that have been neglected in the past, but they are part of a regeneration programme or an upcoming area, where properties are still affordable. At any point you have to make sure that there are reliable transport modes available, so your guests will travel easily back and forth to tourist attractions. It is worthwhile checking local public records, as you will find out exactly what is happening, when and where. Each government will have development plans published by the local council and this is where you should start your search. It is an exciting exercise and, please, do not hesitate to ask questions while there; make a note of all the answers to set the facts right and leave no room for confusion. Keep your findings accurate and up-dated.

Perhaps, your own residential area is the best place to start investing. You already have a taste of the local trends, annual events, your neighbours and local business owners. After all, there will be plenty of mutual benefits as your short term rental will attract more visitors to your home place. You may be able to source a good deal when a neighbour is moving home.

X.2. Second property

You will turn your first property into a delicious commodity for travelers, demand will rise in a very short spin of time, and you will have enough bookings to fill more than one property. When success kicks in, you will see that there is a lot more to your rental property when part of the hospitality industry. Your little business will expand and it will mushroom as an organic need. Soon enough, you will be creating jobs for your family and friends, and because success is contagious, they will join you and in no time, your single property investment will become a small portfolio, and, yes, you are absolutely right to proudly say: 'The Hotel Alternative is my Family Business now!' From here, it is up to you to decide where to go, and when to stop.

Your first property was an exciting project and once you start planning your next step, your second property it will be even easier. You already know everything there is to know about the hospitality industry. You already know best local suppliers you need for your business and you already have a routine, and can decide what to do with your time and when. Having your second property next door to the first one, it is an absolute bliss.

People helping you will have more hours, everything will grow suddenly and saving with your new buying power, picking up bargains everywhere you go, will make your bank manager very happy. Even more, now you can drop your rates because your real profits are coming from volume. Setting your expectations high is not a painful exercise anymore, because, your massive 730 nights a year will generate enough capital to buy your next property with confidence, hire more people, free yourself and enjoy life.

Successful Family run business is all about our ability to pass it on to the next generation. An estimated three million of my country's 4.6 million small firms are run by families. Family Businesses are the backbone of any economy in the world. Entrepreneurs like you and me could feel alienated at times and I am calling you to be part of the incredible quiet force creating jobs and attracting more visitors to our town, city or village. Your community, big or small, depends on your courage to develop new ideas and create wealth.

X.3. Family portfolio

Sourcing further property stock to create availability for demand which is coming from your existing business and good reputation could become your biggest challenge. Being overwhelmed by demand, your greatest difficulty is to increase property stock in good time to fulfill demand. With only one exception, when I was left with empty properties during the Olympic Games because everybody avoided London, I missed massive opportunities due to lack of property stock.

Building your portfolio should not be difficult with such great demand for our product but in downturn economic times it could be virtually impossible to move in the right direction. Perhaps, developing your existing property into few units is a good idea if you are able to buy another residential property for yourself.

Thinking on your feet, when there is no support from your bank and too much business to send away, acquiring property stock is an organic need, not a choice. You could start thinking outside the box, perhaps, and consider working with your family or their capital.

Your immediate family, your children, your friends, they are your network support and JV with them is worth considering.

I know how complicated ownership could be, but working with your family and expanding your portfolio together is best option that I know of and it is working in my case. Joining forces with your nearest and dearest is a very powerful decision and should you be lucky enough to have a family ready to understand your business aspirations, it will be no stopping for your growth.

***

X.4. Succession management

The magic words are: less debt, fiscally focused, succession planning

Taking your family business forward means mastering your skills to achieve unique objectives to future successes and diversification. Family run businesses are mainly about your ability to pass it on to the next generation. Regardless of their size, family businesses need to be planning their management succession from the day they begin trading. Ask the feedback of younger family members regarding your exit from the day to day running of the business at the very beginning.

Succession planning is a tool which will allow your firm to go further, longer and be more successful. Family business could generate billions in sales alone. There are unlimited channels to grow and flourish an innovative concept or a new business idea. Perpetuating your original values will conserve your abilities to trade to your best endeavors.

Most owners are not considering the succession management, either because they are too busy handling existing challenges, or they do not trust their future enough to plan ahead beyond their active involvement. To become the victim of your own success is very easy and you let your expanding business down by having no one to take over your legacy.

In the United Kingdom alone (a small island, after all!) almost three million small firms are run by families. Even we don't get the recognition or assistance we deserve, we truly are Extra Ordinary people, the needed fresh blood of any economic recovery, leading to the future wealth of next generation in both our family and in our society.

Generators of wealth of any country, Family businesses have the need to be nurtured and assisted in every way possible. However, do not expect anyone else to believe in our family business values unless you give it all, in a 100 percent formula of commitments, efforts and sacrifices throughout your active life. Governments seeking economic growth should not underestimate the importance of the family run firms which are absolutely linked to the future health of any economy.

In America, family-controlled businesses account for 35% of Fortune 500 companies and 50% of U.S. gross domestic product. They generate 60% of the country's employment and 78% of all new job creation. In Germany, family businesses contribute to 49% of GDP and only 31% in the United Kingdom.

Latest trend unfolding amongst the Family business is the Daughter Power. Woman-owned family businesses have increased by 37% in the last five years, apparently they are less debt orientated, fiscally conservative, and focused on succession planning, comparing with male-owned businesses. According to experts studying this subject round the world, allowing a woman leadership could save most family business that are otherwise struggling.

Only one in five family businesses makes it past second generation of ownership. Most are sold long before they reach their true potential because there is not enough experience within the family to take the business forward.

X.5. Your legacy for success

What true success means to you could be different from one person to the other. However different, success will manifest and it will start to appear in your life, one way or the other: your normal working hours will decrease and while in the driving seat, you will manage your own time, you will finally find the time for activities that you love. The summit of success is when you are able to allow new, healthy relationships, both with other people and your money, to enter your life. For some property investors, the success they already have in their life is only money and really all there is to achieve in life. Even if you belong to this category, you may feel that something vitally important is missing from your life. Are you ready to try and find what you are missing by letting your energy to burst and surface to new dimensions of satisfaction?

While running your property as The Hotel Alternative you will connect with people that have travelled the world and you will find an abundance of support coming to you from the world itself, a source of positive connections as you move along. You suddenly wake up one morning with an epiphany: money is not everything you can achieve; being connected is what you really want to have in your life.

From what I understand from hundreds of property investors, it could be difficult to achieve personal satisfaction as well as wealth. The realities could be too harsh at times, and, being unattached emotionally could bring more harm than good. For most, success holds no fulfilment, but with The Hotel Alternative, they found the wisdom to redefine success in their own terms.

The road to success should hold a constant appeal, and should support personal growth from inside out, and, mainly, should turn you on, constantly. Welcoming people to your home will bring both financial success and personal fulfilment. Hospitality is a 'people to people' business and opportunities will start knocking on your door. Demand for your residential place is growing at incredible rates, and great visionary minds are working together to create another dimension to the whole travel experience which is called Trip Advisor.

A charismatic person yourself, no doubt, you will sustain the challenge with your energy and enthusiasm, lead your family fortune straight into success, and your bank account will level your heart!

Newcomers to the hospitality industry, we hold great advantages and a competitive edge against current players like hotels, regardless their location or themed luxuries provided as a package. We provide our guests with a real residential home and not a commercial space that you have to imagine is your home, we offer the keys to a real front door and not a room number.

Where hotels are failing, we are winning, simply, because our product is the result of demand and consumers' choice. Making a huge difference in our customers' travel experience, both financially and emotionally, The Hotel Alternative has the ultimate advantage of being conducted directly by professional property owners who are passionate about providing an authentic, well placed concept.

Appendix I

Free listing platform

for your rental property

A.I.1

Keeping the sharing spirit real!

Memorable phrase:

"It's easy to forget sometimes in this technology driven society that behind every tweet, comment and click through is a REAL person." James Blute (Online Strategist for Entrepreneurs).

My best gift to you is the Holly Grail of the hotel alternative's features and benefits: free listing of your property on my marketing platform where, once logged in, your property will go live in 3 easy steps.

Get in touch with me, and I will list your property within my distribution channels so your property will attract immediate audience and your guests will place their booking with you, live. Your guests will make a real payment and you will confirm their booking, in real time, all done... on-line.

Because I am a property owner myself, I understand all difficulties and issues you face when renting your property. I can help with the day to day running of your listing, as well as offering you further help and advice on how to maximize your rental income by listing your property on my e-marketing platform.

We are all part of a virtual space that changed the map of our own spirituality, forever. Most of our guests are making their reservations by using the "Book now button" on-line, as a new style of travelling and part of a sophisticated reality.

There is no way back to the Era of landline telephone numbers when, after 5.00 PM, everybody goes home. We are, all, deeply involved with a Right Now Era.

During my visits to Japan I could not see anyone talking on the phone, as you would in United Kingdom. Instead, everybody was profoundly involved with their phones' screens. I was wondering what was that they were typing into their phones constantly? I understand now and this is the new reality we live in: digital communication.

This is good especially for our business; our clients are busy people, coming from all over the world and because of the time zone differences, digital communication is made very rarely by phone and mainly by e-mail.

I always think twice before making a call, knowing that the person I want to talk to, right now, may be driving, may be in a meeting, on a plane, or, anywhere in the world, where they might even be still asleep.

Actually, on a second thought, I do text instead of calling, or, even better, e-mail. Everything is electronically designed and "e" stands for Extraordinary!

Travelers will choose your house to rent, instead of the most extraordinary hotel room, have no doubts!

What would stop you to offer your rental property as an alternative to hotels and put your property on the map? Few things, which are all related with lack of control over your booking system and the logistic behind it all.

There are a few mistakes I made years back, being genuinely convinced that all I needed to do is to get ready for occupancy. I learned from it. Trust me. We are not a hotel. Most agencies are using a hotel booking system and your three or four bedroom house will be listed as a...room. Of course, you will not appear on the first page during the search, your price will appear to be higher, (and that is ridiculous!) as there is no way of knowing that you are not renting a “room” but an apartment, with a kitchen, bathroom, living room, bedroom and garden!

People will arrive from another continent and they will be shocked to see there is no reception, no hotel signs outside. If you manage to show them around before they go away, their surprise experience will go even further when they will discover that, actually, they don't share a room in your house, but they have the whole property!

Perhaps they will not speak your language and you will not have an interpreter around, so using your body language could help.

From what I know, at this point, you need a miracle for things to go well. There are hundreds of booking agencies and they all want your property on their listings. They will be sweet and convincing, telling you how well you will do once you sign up with them. For some you pay a one off fee, each year, while others are commissioned based.

The more popular and effective they are the higher their annual fee, with prices from as little as $50 to as high as $1500. I can tell you right now that you are better off not parting with your money, regardless of what they peach.

Yes, you will learn how to use their calendar and up-date your availability. However, each agency will generate only between 2-10% of your occupancy, and you will have no choice but to add your property to as many websites as possible, to cover your vacancies.

Sometimes I signed up because I felt that it was worth giving a try and the young person on the phone will not get paid unless they made the sale. But this is not only about the money.

Advertising is linked with your expectations, your cash flow and projections and, most importantly, with other people's travelling plans!

One of two things will happen when you advertise your properties with more than one agency: double bookings or chaos.

How are you going to handle a situation where people are left without accommodation, most of the time, families with kids, arriving at your property after a very late flight, in the middle of the night, not because you accepted a booking in top of another booking, but purely because an agency forced a reservation into their system, very last minute, without you knowing?

What if, somebody from a call centre will make you responsible for it, because they want their commission, regardless?

What if, you have nobody to reason with and you are left with six confused people, in front of your door, hopelessly waiting for a solution from you, because you are the only person and address they have right now and nowhere to go?

I would like you to take the benefit of "going against the wall" years when I had no options but to fight my way out of the dark, thinking that there must be a better way, there must be more to it!

After almost a decade of trying every single agency that there is out there, after paying every single penny left on fees I should not have paid, because nothing came out of them anyway, after paying the hotel bill for guests I have never accepted the reservation for, to start with, after being completely lost and feeling totally alienated, I decided to find the right solution for my business model. I am not blaming anyone but myself!
Very few of the agencies I have been working with during the last decade gained my respect and admiration for their ethics. I am still listing properties with those few agencies whom I have admiration for due to their marketing strategies.

We worked together to find “the one solution” that allows us to share our availability calendar, so there will be no double bookings, or misunderstandings for that matter. Both my sons worked tirelessly, for years, to discover the holly grail of our booking system, that unique solution for our business model, which allows you and me to list our properties live, and accurately, up-date our availability, in less than 2 minutes.

When they started their discovery journey, my sons wanted to free up my time and help me work smart. I was working an average of 14 hours a day and had no holidays or weekends at the time. Now I am free to travel and enjoy my life again, I do not carry two phones with me anymore as I used to even when I was taking the dogs for a walk, nor do I write hundreds of e-mails daily to reply to enquiries.

I am ever grateful for my sons' unconditional support and enthusiasm over the years! I hope you will greatly enjoy the benefit of working smart!

As a big *Thank You!* for buying my book, you can list your property, free of charge, on my website, whether your house to rent is an apartment in the city or a remote cottage, anywhere in the whole world! Listing your properties for free, as a standalone bonus, will save you at least five figures marketing costs! You will have the perfect platform for your properties, at your fingertips!

Do you have a house for rent, anywhere in the world? I would love to help you double your rental income, recession or no recession. Most investment properties will bring you wealth when let on a short-term basis.

I am confidently opening the gates for you. Please step in now and add your own mark to the hospitality market. My business model on successful property rental was designed with you in mind, regardless the type of your property. Should you decide to talk to me about your holiday homes, I will assess your property, and if I consider that our existing clients and prospective guests will benefit, I will start promoting your place and make sure that you will see an immediate cash flow boost!

AI.2.

Go live in 3 steps!

1.

Guests log onto the website and place enquiries for your property.

2.

1. You confirm availability.
or
2. Use "live booking" for instant reservations.

3.

The booking is confirmed and payment is collected.

Welcome your guests and receive your rent.

Your Property Listing with Away from Home, the Hotel Alternative benefits and features:

- Completely free to list when you buy the book "Away From Home –The Hotel Alternative, a complete guide for Home Owners and their rental properties"
- You set your daily rates and have full control of your bookings, you approve or decline first
- Set your damage security deposit and get piece of mind when renting your property
- Full payment and damage security deposit collected at the time of booking
- Payments released to you; tested payment structure protects owners and guests alike
- Payments sent from UK bank accounts - balances settle the same day
- Highly versatile platform with private owners area (allows full control of your listing)
- Access your profile from anywhere in the world, using a pc, tablet or smart phone
- View reservations, availability and enquiries, guests' reports, vacancies and income, plus much more!
- Email Parsing allows you to respond to enquiries in just a few clicks
- Full property profile to including; up to 20 photos, local area and property description, cancellation policy, amenities and much more
- Add live availability calendars and enquiry forms to your own website or blog with ease

The Platform/ benefits to you

- Cross platform for distribution channels and all major international rental websites
- We are already connected to most popular relocation and holiday portals, with more being added all the time
- Control your calendars from a single location, even from your iPhone
- Keep your availability up to date and synchronized with your existing listings
- Minimize your workload; eliminate double bookings and stay fully booked
- Active marketing to thousands of high quality existing guests
- Free property profile newsletter sent to our mailing list consisting of thousands of previous clients
- Free front-page feature for 1 week upon joining
- Free photo shoot to present your property in the best light possible

AI.3.

The power of social media

Building your business is a complex process of making the right decision, at the right time, for the right reasons.

Marketing your property is not only about creating a webpage and opening few social media accounts. Learning from other people's mistakes and not repeating your own will help you go from strength to strength. Being open and sharing your experiences is the fabric of knowing how to grow in a sophisticated travel market driven by consumer choice.

After lots of thinking on the saga of mobile communication and negotiating with myself "should I, should I not write about the power of social media", I decided to share with you everything there is to know about The Power of Social Media and your rental property.

At first, it seemed like an unnecessary diversion from what I do and what I am good at. Then, just recently, I started my Twitter, and really enjoyed being connected with people I have never met before but with similar interests.

Then I started meeting them, in real life, and I feel that my whole wellbeing is so much richer now! Sharing other peoples' knowledge and genius, added a new dimension to my work environment, made it more exciting, in a way that makes me... click.

If still in the dark, like I was, I hope you will discover the Spirit of Sharing too!

Nothing new for most of you, if you are like my kids, but if you are like me, the vintage type, who believes in all there is as real and solid, like bricks and mortar, and prefers a real smile to 1000's of emoticons, please make this discovery journey complete, and open the gates of Social Media with both your arms.

There are shortcuts which you would like to learn about, from social media authorities, bloggers, really smart guys ready to reveal invaluable knowledge to you; please have a look on Google (or click for that matter).

Most wanted tools are already at your fingertips, to experience my business model and free for you to access new clients and new business from all over the world.

Adding visibility to your rental home through social media channels could be time consuming, and time is the one commodity that none of us is willingly giving up.

Think of social media as an aphrodisiac that you could share with your friends and "clients to be". Talking about the miracles of World Wide Web, I have met, online, hundreds of people who are sharing their published work with passion and enthusiasm.

Disregarding Social Media is not a mistake, but a cardinal sin, as you are basically closing the gates to thousands of potential customers. In figures, this means that 64% of people on Twitter are buying from brands they follow.

Your presence on Twitter alone will increase your sales revenue and bring fresh business in, based on the simple fact that you are on the same platform and your visibility is amplified by the Voice of your own customers.

Twitter is my favorite channel. It is short and sweet; all messages are restricted to 140 characters and that is more than enough for good communication.

Like yourself, my time is very limited, and I do not have an office to work from, but I do have an iPhone and "there is an app for everything". Since I installed the Twitter app, I am truly connected and all I need is to tweet or RT to be part of Right Now. I am absolutely convinced that Tweeter is one marketing tool that is costing only your time and enthusiasm.

Creating your brand with consistence and being present for your followers' developments and events in a steady, unselfish way, it will create a loyal audience you can, too, rely on. The voice of your own customer will affect your small business profitability and growth both "right now" and on a long term.

Of course, you can choose any social media channel and perhaps, it is best to have at least two favourites, just in case one of your accounts will close, you are still live on the other. Remember that you should try to communicate with your followers directly and be able to e-mail them if you have mutual interests. However, being live on too many platforms, could eat up your time, or get your loyalties spreading too thin.

So, what is to know about Social Media that is not said yet? Personally I believe that Social Media it is both, the Spirit of Sharing itself, and a RIGHT NOW phenomenon. Should you dare to join and go live, the Power of Communication is yours, to share. The master key to your success is putting across the right message, at the right time, to the right people. Most experts consider the social media boom over and that is all right because, from our point of view, as property investors, the World Wide Web is just starting. There are 2 billion users and you need to be out there to reach them!

A.I.4

Why you should go blogging

Blogs are part of the search engine algorithms and because of this, marketing your home rental means creating your own brand and be live on the World Wide Web.
On your blog, you can add further information about yourself, your family photos, videos and your guests' testimonials. You can list your property's features, your local area guide, on a sequenced delivery, articles from local media, sportive events, art fairs, celebrities coming to your town, anything that is connected to your property that will raise an interest to your clients- to- be.

You can do special blog posts, for example, a special offer as part as a celebration or Festival that is going to take place in your local area. You can offer a special discount for their stay to all participants, in consideration for the benefits and fame they bring to your area.

Writing your blog is very dynamic and you should use catchy phrases, don't be afraid of creating new meanings to old sayings, or connect with other bloggers anywhere in the world. People will leave a comment on your blog, which makes it all very interesting on a two ways street. No website or e-mail can create the interaction you need, like a good blog.

You could always keep the momentum going by adding a link to your special offer, where people can make their reservation online, then and there.

You can blog about your guests and their stay as long as there are 500- 800 exciting words with feed back through comments and reviews on their stay. Perhaps, the shop round the corner told you that they had record sales since you start running your hotel alternative home and they are back on track with their own business.

Good news will travel fast! You will attract traffic on related topics and similar subjects. Your sales page or BOOK NOW button will allow your visitors to place their reservation just when they finish reading your blog.

Gradually you will build an audience and People can subscribe to your blog through an RSS feed. You can build relationships with these people and get direct feedback.

Blogging enables you to build a personal marketing platform where you create your own brand, brick by brick, as well as your online presence. Your intimate knowledge of the local area will create your authority and your own audience. To understand the power of blogging, you should sink in with the technological truth: each time you post another blog, you are creating new exciting pages for your website.

Google, from the other hand, updates your web content, which is indexed; as a result, you end up building a growing presence for your rental property and more and more people will find you during their search

Appendix II

Ask the experts

With Big Thanks to everyone who answered my questions and helped create this page. The purpose of this Appendix is to share with you my outsourced information and to present you with answers on hot topics:

property experts opinions on property market,

what are booking agents doing to bring in the business for you

what social media authorities will recommend for marketing your property

I only selected the following interviews, which I believe will help you the most.

(There are just first names attached to the experts I interviewed purely because this is not a platform for their promotion but a source of useful information for yourself.)

AII.1.

Interview with Matt, Property Investor (UK)

Q1:Is the desire for buying property stagnant for our young generation?

A1: *Young Owners occupiers are in an impossible mission and for somebody in their late twenties or early thirties, to go and buy a property, it is just an aspiration at present. The only way adult children can have their own property is ...to rent from their parents. Considering that 32,200 loans worth £3,700,000 are buy-to-let borrowings this year, 2012 remains at about a third of 2007's position. Even with the deposits of minimum of 75%, parents have to go back to the housing market as buy-to-let property investors because their children struggle to get on the property ladder and buy their own property. There is a strong desire, but no real solution for the younger generation, which leads me, as a parent, to further commit and take on even more liabilities, when I should plan my retirement!*

Q2: How is the Buy-to-let market changing and what are your intentions as a property investor?

A2: *There is a significant rise in buy-to-let borrowings, which reflects the demand for rental property, as a result of mortgage funds being out of reach for owners occupiers. In my opinion, the first-time buyers are being squeezed out of the property market.*

The map of the whole property market is changing as we speak, purely because the lending criteria are dictating the consumer behavior's trend. House prices are stagnant in some postcodes or falling in others, depending on who lives there.

There are deals to have but I would take a long view on any property purchase because, after I had my own short term play and lost, I learned that could be very dangerous when you don't have a ten years plan.

I would also buy a freehold property with minimum three or four bedrooms, because people do not plan any more to move again each couple of years. Younger generations stay with their families for longer as they need years to save money to buy their own place and, as a result, there is a shortage on supply for family houses.

My lender helped me get back on track when I experienced difficulties and I had to work very hard to keep up my monthly payments with tenants not able to pay their rent. I understand that the number of mortgages in arrears fell overall but personally, I keep an open mind and my eyes are wide opened on my finances. I will never let my properties on an Assured Tenancy Agreement, again. Giving a license to live to tenants is what got me into trouble to start with, and renting my properties with a new business model, as alternative to hotels, is the only option I will ever consider. It is not only that the rental income is at least double, but I am in control of my finances, I can plan ahead for long term, taking the benefits of short term rentals.

Q3: What are your expectations on interest rates movements?

***A3:** Right now, with inflation at 3.5pc, we have to brace ourselves for deeper recession. The interest rates are still record low and, hopefully, they will not rise until 2013- 2014 at the earliest, as the UK's growth is not anywhere near Bank's predicted level. Growth is endangered by fast price raising and a stagnant economy and for many families the living standards are affected badly by the high level of inflation and economic downturn. Paying the price for the period of boom is now a reality hard to ignore. I am not an analyst and it is the Banks' job to keep inflation down. I would keep a long-term view on any investment.*

Q4: What is your view on the property market in 2012-the year of Diamond Jubilee?

A4: *Very simply, in the last 60 years, average house prices have rocketed, 100 fold.I read that average UK property prices have increased 16 times since the Silver Jubilee celebrations in 1977 and over 100 times since the Queen's Coronation in 1952.In 1952 the average price of a UK home was just £1,520, £9,737 in 1977 and £160,000 in 2012. In other words, any property price increases at an average of £7 per day! Of course, in London, property prices are rocketing from £2,650 to £354,300 since the Coronation year, which is an actual increase of 134 times.*

With the help of Government, there are schemes where you can make your money go further. If you want to buy their first home or move to a bigger property, you pay only 5% deposit. Your dream home is still there waiting for you!

After all, our love for bricks and mortar is genetic and 2012 is here to prove that investing in property is the most reliable investment for any of us.

AII.2.

Interview with Celine,

from Local Nomad, International Booking Agency

Q1: What will give you the edge over other agencies?

We are specialized in high standard apartments, luxurious villas and apart hotel.

We have a real qualified customer service in 7 languages open 7 days a week. Each destination has one destination manager, owners' support and between 1 to 3 agents to inform the clients (customer and quality service). We give special attention to each guest; by calling to confirm they are having a good stay and or sending them a survey at the end of their stay.

During the collaboration with property owners, we handle all the advertisement and reservation processes, subject to homeowner's approval.

Q2: Are tourists and accommodation seekers using the Internet to book their holiday rentals?

The Internet is the only communication channel we are using.

Most of our clients find us through Google and others have already used our services and want to reproduce the experience for their next trip.

Q3: What kind of properties are they looking to, for their stay?

Our clients contact us to find a good quality accommodation that is well located. They want a fully equipped accommodation with a kitchen to get the feeling of home. We also have business travelers who prefer apartments to hotels.

Q4: How can you strategically market a property for best exposure worldwide?

There are currently various ways of achieving good online exposure worldwide. Good online presence allows clients better access to all our properties. Therefore, the marketing team works on different aspects in order to increase exposure on the SERP (Search Engine Result Pages):

1. Search Engine Optimization (Website is reached via the main and most important keywords) e.g. "location, apartments, London": 1st page, 1st position on Google

2. Ad words advertising (Display campaigns targeting specific markets)

3. Social networks (Facebook, Twitter etc.): We need to be present on social networks as they are included in the search engine algorithms, thus the more popular we are and the more people are aware of our brand, the more chance we have of appearing in the search engines.

4. Blogs: A branding blog to promote our brand and products

Moreover, we are part of a network of companies specializing in online real estate and reservation services. Therefore, working with one company within the group implies access to a database of more than 100,000 customers, and online presence in 5 languages on the 13 other websites belonging to the group.

Q5: What is the definition of Owners Support in your company philosophy?

We give a lot of importance to our owners from the moment we contact them to propose our services to becoming our partners.

We offer them the best visibility online as we can, spending for that every year 35% of our benefits.

We both have the same interest in regards to renting the properties(s) as frequent as possible. In Routine, the destination manager will contact the owner/ property manager by telephone or via email to suggest ways to bring in more booking, For example: to propose to make the properties(s) more attractive, to set up an offer, to put better quality pictures and advising prices.

Our customer service agent, if necessary, will help our owners to be in contact with the clients regarding their advance fee payment, the check in and checkout time, or with a cancellation.

There is one calendar support agent in who is in charge of manually updating the calendars and to confirm that all partners are consistently updating their calendars.

We also have a quality customer service that makes sure each client enjoys their stay. In the case of a complaint, we ask the version of each party (client and owner) to clarify the situation, to help them in finding a mutual agreement.

Q6: Having this year's experience for London Olympics 2012, what would be, the top three tips you could give to Home Owners in Rio de Janeiro, which will host the Olympic Games 2016, en exactly 1.547 days*?

Regarding the Olympics Games in Rio de Janeiro I would suggest:

- Set your rates two times or maximum three times the normal price but no more, otherwise there will not be any bookings.

- Change the prices depending on the occupancy; if you have a lot of availability don't hesitate to lower the prices.

- Compare the prices with the competitors to make sure your prices are attractive.

** Interview was taken in May 2012*

AII.3.

Winning attributes of top bloggers by Chris, International Blogger Authority

Hi Marina,

Think about your favorite blogs, what separates them from the rest?

Some bloggers succeed at attracting an audience. They build a brand, reputation, respect. They get the attention. At the same time, there are other bloggers looking up at those blogs saying "Why are they different?" Here are the winning attributes of the top bloggers:

1. They put readers first - Give first, the rewards come after you have created value for your readers. At all times your audience should be central to everything you do, both in your writing and in every experience of dealing with you.

2. They have something to say - Rather than recycling and linking an Authority Blogger will create, will add their thoughts and ideas, will share the benefit of their experience.

3. They maintain quality - When things get hard it is easy to slip into "barely good enough" but you must always strive for the best quality you can maintain. Some bloggers slip when they find a bit of success, like they don't have to try. Nobody is perfect, but if your quality slips don't expect your audience to stick around.

4. They build relationships - No blog is an island, and even the top bloggers rely on others from time to time. Get out into the blog world and make yourself known and a valued member of the web.

5. They are unique - You have to stand out. Give people good reasons to talk about you. Be different in a beneficial way. Not just a novelty but remarkable in a way that is useful. You might gain a much bigger initial audience and traffic by being noticed in more controversial ways but that is not the way to build long-term and substantial value.

None of these things are particularly easy, but they are essential for success.

Plan now to bring these attributes into your own blogging and watch your audience, loyalty and credibility grow.

Cheers, Chris

Appendix III

Don't break the red tape

AIII.1. Health and Safety

When you welcome visitors coming to stay with you, as a landlord, you are responsible for their health and safety during their stay at your property

While your visitors have a duty to use your property in a responsible way as they signed an agreement to do so, you are the host and you have to ensure that your property is well equipped and maintained. Your guests will be responsible to keep clear kitchen sinks and made sure that are not clogged of food waste, to avoid blockages, and for any damage caused by their family or friends during their stay at your property. They should not carry out repairs to your property, but call the Duty Manager number you provided them instead, at the time of check in. It is always important to handle that telephone in such way that all emergency calls are answered prompt and in good time.

You have to be the first person satisfied with your Gas and Electric equipment and make sure they are safely installed and maintained in good working order at all times. Your main objective is to keep your property and their occupants safe from any hazard. For example, carrying out your own checks for potential hazards, like damp, would give peace of mind that no accident could occur while you are not present. Each country has local rules but, you must follow fire safety regulation as a common sense habit and check that your guests have access to escape routes at all times, remove any eventual blockages and clearly explain all exits available at check in time. You may leave a direction to exits map on the internal side of your main entrance door.

In general, an annual maintenance check for your gas and electrical installation and also for existing appliances carried out by an authorized engineer registered with the Gas Safe Register, depending where your property is located, would give you good re-assurance that you are providing a safe environment to your guests.

Most countries will have similar building rules and regulations to protect occupants from fire hazard that could harm. Your property will normally have fire doors and clear fire escapes. As a Landlord, you have to make sure that your furniture is fire-resistant. Furniture manufacturers will usually label their fire-resistant products and choosing those suppliers for your furniture; will help your piece of mind on the long run; because your property is let on short-term basis, fire regulations do not apply.

AIII.2. Tax pages round the world

I gathered little information that I really hope you will find useful and easy to read. For further up-to date news on this subject, please e-mail me with your questions and I will find an expert to answer and help you with your enquiry.

This is a wide open subject, and various groups in various countries are organising petitions to change unfair rules and regulations, as we speak, while other governments are trying to help grow their local economy by relaxing rules, engaging with entrepreneurs and encouraging tourism.

In the United Kingdom, Her Majesty The Queen, is an extraordinary visionary mind and she always encourages and supports entrepreneurs to invest in property, and there are rules in place that protect the interest of property owners who run furnished property lettings. My personal opinion is that anyone that wants to invest in the property market, should definitely invest in the United Kingdom.

United Kingdom and European Economic Area

Finance Act 2011 s 52 and s 14 is bringing three specific changes to the furnished holiday letting rules that apply for income tax and corporation tax purposes, because the original furnished holiday letting rules were in breach of EU law.

The rules now apply to all properties in the UK and the European Economic Area and are regarded as two separate properties (income and corporation tax purposes). In short, these changes are related to qualifying criteria, loss relief, and extension of the rules to properties in the European Economic Area (EEA). The original furnished holiday letting rules (introduced in FA 1984) were restricted to UK properties only. The lengths of periods for which the accommodation must be available for letting and for which it must be actually let are both extended.

The previous limits were that property must be available for letting for 140 days and actually let for 70 days. These are to be extended to 210 and 105 days respectively. This change takes effect for income tax purposes from 2012/13 and for corporation tax purposes for accounting periods ending on or after 1 April 2012.

For income tax purposes the changes take effect from 2011/12 and for corporation tax purposes for accounting periods beginning on or after 1 April 2011.

There are a few tax implications for Furnished Holiday Lettings in the UK and EEA, which will help you work out your taxable profit. To calculate, simply total your deductible expenses and subtract them from your rental income. Please make a note of your allowable expenses such as: utility bills, council tax, cleaning and linen services paid for, phone calls, advertising and stationery, booking agent fees, legal fees, accountant fees, insurance, interest on mortgage payments, maintenance and repair costs.

For the tax years 2010/11 and 2011/12, in addition to the capital allowances for furniture and other equipment you may also be able to claim up to 25 per cent or more of the original purchase price of the property as a tax allowance or capital allowance based on the integral features of the property.

Your accountant will know exactly how to advise on the amount you claim each year, as this does vary from year to year and greatly depends on new government policies. I am not an expert and I could not possible give you advise but I could introduce you to my accountant should you not have one available. Best is to look for an accountant specialized on Furnished Property Lettings. This is a complex subject, but have no fear, a good accountant will be able to look into your personal circumstances and advise you on your benefits when letting a furnished property.

United States

In the United States, you should be aware of zoning regulations that are affecting how you use your property when letting to paying guests. Different states will have different regulations and it is very important to check the zoning rules for your property. It is meant to balance the development of a town with the general public interest at heart, for the best outcome for the entire community as a whole. To be used different part of a community in various ways, they must be divided in zones, such as: residential, commercial, industrial and agriculture.

As a holiday homes owner, you may experience restrictions on short let in a residential zone or in zones for single family homes, to preserve the full enjoyment of property owners who reside at the property.

Check your property type of zone and subzones, which could overrule town regulations; each development has its own zoning rules, which will allow you to rent your property and for how long. As not knowing it is not an excuse, checking with your local authorities if you are allowed to rent and if, so, for how long you will be avoiding severe penalties. As a property owner you can request changes to the existing use during public hearings. Amendments can be made if such changes are in the best interest of the community. Otherwise, you can request a special permit and a "Spot Zoning" for your particular property location will be issued, subject to the public's best interest. Define that! Best is to do your homework prior to purchasing your property.

There are few countries where I could assist your property purchase because I know the inside out of the local rules and cultural trends, but, as I said already, personally, I would only make an investment in the United Kingdom.

Appendix IV

Take the fear out of finance

AIV.1

Cash flow model

Please see attachment Turnover- Large House converted in 4 units

Example: Cash flow for large house that was converted in 4 units

i. Actual turnover is always higher than projected at the mentioned occupancy levels. This is due to extra charges mentioned above (e.g. extra guests) and peak periods (e.g Easter bank holiday in April).

ii. The months of July and August will see traditionally higher turnover as demand grows from holiday makers and visitors.

iii. At current levels the property is set to achieve a turnover that is 30% higher overall than projected figures for each occupancy level.

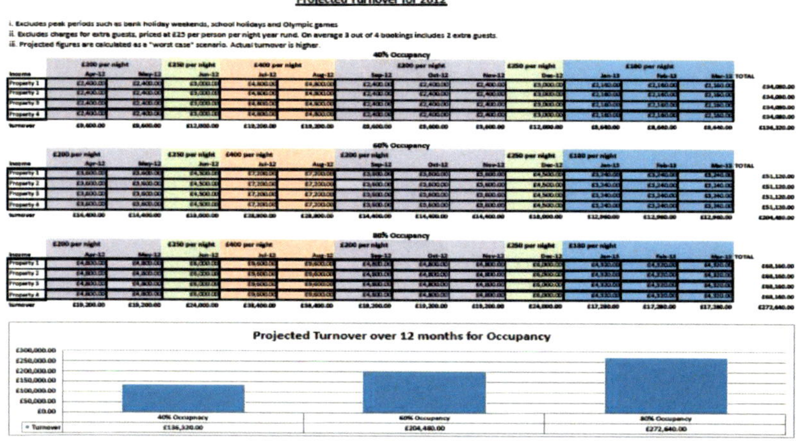

Projected Turnover for 2012

i. Excludes peak periods such as bank holiday weekends, school holidays and Olympic games
ii. Excludes charges for extra guests, priced at £25 per person per night year rund. On average 3 out of 4 bookings includes 2 extra guests.
iii. Projected figures are calculated as a "worst case" scenario. Actual turnover is higher.

40% Occupancy

Income	£200 per night		£250 per night	£400 per night		£200 per night			£250 per night	£180 per night			
	Apr-12	May-12	Jun-12	Jul-12	Aug-12	Sep-12	Oct-12	Nov-12	Dec-12	Jan-13	Feb-13	Mar-13	TOTAL
Property 1	£2,400.00	£2,400.00	£3,000.00	£4,800.00	£4,800.00	£2,400.00	£2,400.00	£2,400.00	£3,000.00	£2,160.00	£2,160.00	£2,160.00	£34,080.00
Property 2	£2,400.00	£2,400.00	£3,000.00	£4,800.00	£4,800.00	£2,400.00	£2,400.00	£2,400.00	£3,000.00	£2,160.00	£2,160.00	£2,160.00	£34,080.00
Property 3	£2,400.00	£2,400.00	£3,000.00	£4,800.00	£4,800.00	£2,400.00	£2,400.00	£2,400.00	£3,000.00	£2,160.00	£2,160.00	£2,160.00	£34,080.00
Property 4	£2,400.00	£2,400.00	£3,000.00	£4,800.00	£4,800.00	£2,400.00	£2,400.00	£2,400.00	£3,000.00	£2,160.00	£2,160.00	£2,160.00	£34,080.00
Turnover	£9,600.00	£9,600.00	£12,000.00	£19,200.00	£19,200.00	£9,600.00	£9,600.00	£9,600.00	£12,000.00	£8,640.00	£8,640.00	£8,640.00	£136,320.00

60% Occupancy

Income	£200 per night		£250 per night	£400 per night		£200 per night			£250 per night	£180 per night			
	Apr-12	May-12	Jun-12	Jul-12	Aug-12	Sep-12	Oct-12	Nov-12	Dec-12	Jan-13	Feb-13	Mar-13	TOTAL
Property 1	£3,600.00	£3,600.00	£4,500.00	£7,200.00	£7,200.00	£3,600.00	£3,600.00	£3,600.00	£4,500.00	£3,240.00	£3,240.00	£3,240.00	£51,120.00
Property 2	£3,600.00	£3,600.00	£4,500.00	£7,200.00	£7,200.00	£3,600.00	£3,600.00	£3,600.00	£4,500.00	£3,240.00	£3,240.00	£3,240.00	£51,120.00
Property 3	£3,600.00	£3,600.00	£4,500.00	£7,200.00	£7,200.00	£3,600.00	£3,600.00	£3,600.00	£4,500.00	£3,240.00	£3,240.00	£3,240.00	£51,120.00
Property 4	£3,600.00	£3,600.00	£4,500.00	£7,200.00	£7,200.00	£3,600.00	£3,600.00	£3,600.00	£4,500.00	£3,240.00	£3,240.00	£3,240.00	£51,120.00
Turnover	£14,400.00	£14,400.00	£18,000.00	£28,800.00	£28,800.00	£14,400.00	£14,400.00	£14,400.00	£18,000.00	£12,960.00	£12,960.00	£12,960.00	£204,480.00

80% Occupancy

Income	£200 per night		£250 per night	£400 per night		£200 per night			£250 per night	£180 per night			
	Apr-12	May-12	Jun-12	Jul-12	Aug-12	Sep-12	Oct-12	Nov-12	Dec-12	Jan-13	Feb-13	Mar-13	TOTAL
Property 1	£4,800.00	£4,800.00	£6,000.00	£9,600.00	£9,600.00	£4,800.00	£4,800.00	£4,800.00	£6,000.00	£4,320.00	£4,320.00	£4,320.00	£68,160.00
Property 2	£4,800.00	£4,800.00	£6,000.00	£9,600.00	£9,600.00	£4,800.00	£4,800.00	£4,800.00	£6,000.00	£4,320.00	£4,320.00	£4,320.00	£68,160.00
Property 3	£4,800.00	£4,800.00	£6,000.00	£9,600.00	£9,600.00	£4,800.00	£4,800.00	£4,800.00	£6,000.00	£4,320.00	£4,320.00	£4,320.00	£68,160.00
Property 4	£4,800.00	£4,800.00	£6,000.00	£9,600.00	£9,600.00	£4,800.00	£4,800.00	£4,800.00	£6,000.00	£4,320.00	£4,320.00	£4,320.00	£68,160.00
Turnover	£19,200.00	£19,200.00	£24,000.00	£38,400.00	£38,400.00	£19,200.00	£19,200.00	£19,200.00	£24,000.00	£17,280.00	£17,280.00	£17,280.00	£272,640.00

AIV.2. Management accounts made simple

I have created my own monthly reports by creating simple rules on an Excel spreadsheet and adding all categories I used in real life: Please see two attachments with relevant information for:

Income and Expenditure

Graph

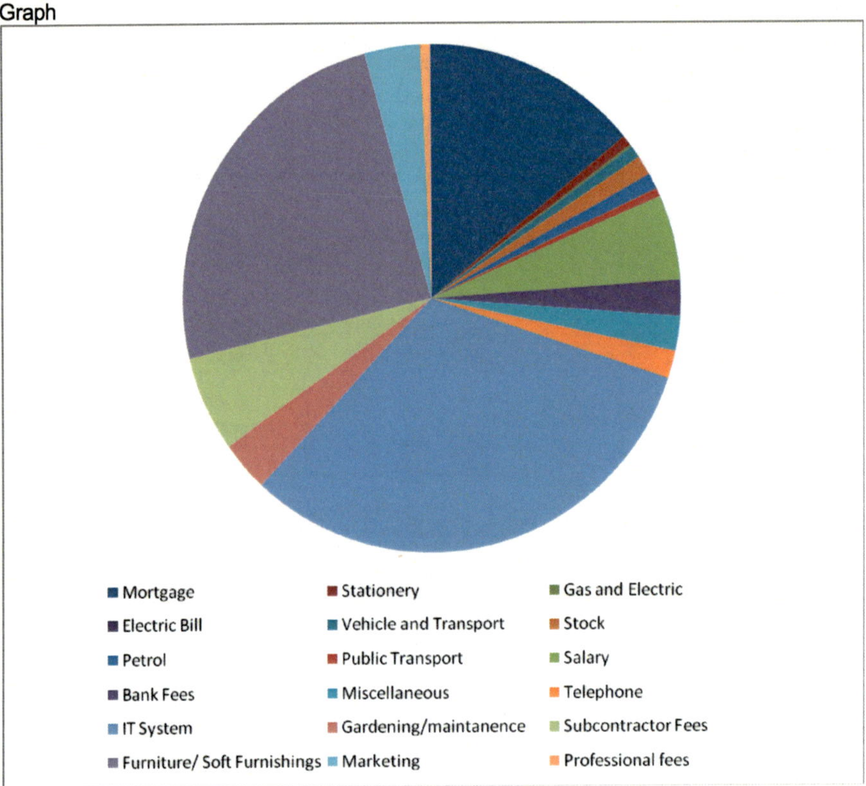

Also, bellow you have a template for Internal Management Accounts

To create your own records for internal management accounts you can simply add categories you use in real life for easy personal records

Date	Expenditure	Description	Amount of Payment

more templates and forms are available from www.AwayFromHome-book.com

Categories:

Mortgage
Rates
Gas and Electric
Water Bill
Vehicle and Transport
Stock
Petrol
Public Transport
Salary
Bank Fees
Miscellaneous
Telephone
IT System
Gardening/maintenance
Subcontractor Fees
Furniture/ Soft
Furnishings
Marketing
Professional fees

AIV.3. Useful Reports and templates

1. Booking Reports

To access your Internal Reports just click on Reports button and chose the relevant dates. Should you choose to start your own manual reports, this is an easy template:

Date	Booking Number	Guest Name	Amount of Payment	Payment Type

2. House Keeping Reports

Once you get into a routine, I found that taking notes and keeping records it will really help to keep an eye on your expenditure, but, most importantly, measure your performances along the way.

Date	Booking Number	Cleaning Agency	Amount of hours	Payment Type

3. Linen and Towels Records

Using local suppliers or hiring local help is very important because you want to put your time at better use. Keeping accurate records for how much linen you use and how much is costing you to provide linen and towels, is part of the weekly routine and helps you calculate your rates. Crispy linen and fresh towels will help your guests enjoy their stay.

Date	Linen/ pillows	towels	Amount of Payment	Payment Type

4. Damage Deposit Report

Personally I do not charge a security deposit but I do take a valid credit card upon arrival and authorize the payment without charging the guests' card. It is too complicated to take refundable payment, but should you choose to, please keep records to make sure you make the refund at the end of stay, at check out time.

Date	Booking Number	Guest Name	Amount of Payment	Payment Type

5. Property Inventory Template

You can find many examples of detailed property inventory templates online. Simple download a template and specify it according to your needs.

Please e-mail me

To request free templates and inventory forms

Marina@AwayFromHome-book.com

Thank you!

'Away from Home- The Hotel Alternative' Program TM

S.A.V.E.
Short-term - Accommodation in a residential area that is -Versatile to your needs and gives you an – Exclusive but economic private living space.

Whilst the book is helping many owners develop new and strong streams of income, the help doesn't end there. There are webinars available, workshop, and weekend VIP Retreats organized all year round, in various locations worldwide.

The series contains many other books, with numerous new titles planned for the future, all in support of property owners joining The Hotel Alternative

In fact, this November sees the launch of

'Away From Home -The Complete Guide for the Savvy World Traveler'

Scheduled to debut in California, many within the industry await the latest title with bated breath. In the meantime, more details about the book, as well as an analysis of The Hotel Alternative Program, can be found online at:

http://www.awayfromhome-book.com